Organizational Video-Ethnography Revisited

Sylvie Grosjean · Frédérik Matte
Editors

Organizational Video-Ethnography Revisited

Making Visible Material, Embodied and Sensory Practices

palgrave
macmillan

Editors
Sylvie Grosjean
Department of Communication
University of Ottawa
Ottawa, ON, Canada

Frédérik Matte
Department of Communication
University of Ottawa
Ottawa, ON, Canada

ISBN 978-3-030-65550-1 ISBN 978-3-030-65551-8 (eBook)
https://doi.org/10.1007/978-3-030-65551-8

This Palgrave Pivot imprint is published by the registered company Springer Nature Switzerland AG
The registered company address is: Gewerbestrasse 11, 6330 Cham, Switzerland

Contents

Notes on Contributors

Nicolas Bencherki is an associate professor of organizational communication at TÉLUQ Montréal, Canada. His work investigates the way communication and materiality constitute organizational reality, including classic notions such as strategy, authority or membership, using ethnographic and action-research approaches. His work has been published, among others, in the *Academy of Management Journal*, *Organization Studies*, *Human Relations*, *Long Range Planning*, *Strategic Organization*, the *Journal of Communication*, and *Communication Theory*.

Jeff Bezemer is Professor of Communication at University College London (UK) and Director of the Centre for Multimodal Research at the UCL Institute of Education. His interests are in social interaction, technology and learning. His research is focused on (video-)ethnographic studies in health care settings, including the operating room, intensive care unit, and ambulance service. Recent books include *Multimodality, Learning and Communication: A Social Semiotic Frame* (with Gunther Kress); and *Introducing Multimodality* (with Carey Jewitt and Kay O'Halloran).

Claudine Bonneau is Associate Professor at UQAM School of Management in Montréal, Canada. She is a member of the Laboratory for Communication and the Digital (LabCMO) and teaches in graduate and undergraduate programs in Information Technology. Her current work focuses on new work practices, social media uses and online collaboration. She is also interested in methodological issues related to qualitative research and online ethnography. Besides her contributions to edited books (such as *Experiencing the New World of Work*, Cambridge University Press, forthcoming, *New Ways of Working: Organizations and Organizing in the Digital Age*, Palgrave Macmillan, forthcoming and the *Handbook of Social Media Research Methods*, Sage, 2017), her work has published in journals such as *Educational Technology Research and Development*, *Communication, Research & Practice* and the *International Journal of Project Management.*

Laurent Filliettaz is Professor of Adult and Vocational Education at the University of Geneva (Switzerland). He is a specialist in discourse analysis and multimodal approaches to interaction. His research is strongly interdisciplinary and combines contributions from applied linguistics and educational sciences. Over the years, he has conducted several empirical research programs on topics such as language use in professional contexts, apprenticeship and interactional competences in vocational education and training.

Sylvie Grosjean is Professor of Organizational Communication and Health Communication at University of Ottawa (Canada) and holder of the International Francophonie Research Chair on Digital Health Technologies. Her current research interests include the design and implementation of telehealth innovations (e.g., telemedicine, mHealth, sensor devices) as well as organizational communication by studying the role of technologies on care coordination and clinical decision-making. She uses qualitative methods (e.g., organizational ethnography, visual methods, narrative interviews, video-ethnography) and she develops co-design/Participatory Design approaches in healthcare settings.

Rick Iedema is professor and director of the Centre for Team-Based Practice & Learning in Health Care at King's College London (UK). His main research interest is in how clinicians collaborate and communicate, and in the ways patients can become involved in healthcare practice improvement.

Michael Jarrett is Professor of Management Practice in Organizational Behavior at INSEAD (European Institute of Business Administration). His research interests focus on the social and political interactions of top management teams and the consequences for strategic decision-making, execution and outcomes. Drawing on the concept of behavioral strategy, his work integrates micro-sociology, organizational theory and psychological theories of implicit affects. He has published a number of books on change management as well as in outlets including *Organizational Research Methods*, *Organizational Dynamics* and *Harvard Business Review*.

Feng Liu is an Assistant Professor at Sobey School of Business, Saint Mary's University (Canada). She received her Ph.D. from the University of British Columbia, Canada. She uses video-based methods in her research on emotion in organizations and board and top management team strategizing activities. Her recent research has been published in *Journal of Management Studies*, *Organizational Research Methods*, and *Strategic Organization*.

Frédérik Matte is Professor of Organizational Communication at University of Ottawa (Canada). He studies tensions in the extreme and emergency situations faced by international non-governmental organizations (INGOs). He is interested in patient caring relationships, organizational change, intercultural settings and multilingual environments, as well as ethical issues. He has published in the *International Journal of Communication*, *Journal of Communication*, *ommunication Monographs*, *Discourse and Communication* and *Pragmatics & Society*.

Jeanne Mengis is Professor of Organizational Communication at the Università della Svizzera italiana (USI, Switzerland), and Honorary Associate Professor at Warwick Business School (UK). Her research is focused on how material actors—such as artifacts or space—mediate organizational and communication practices, in particular knowledge work, innovation and interdisciplinary work.

Isaac Nahón-Serfaty is Professor in the Department of Communication at the University of Ottawa (Canada). He is a scholar, writer and consultant in organizational communication, with extensive experience in health communication, crisis management and corporate social responsibility. He is also interested in studying "sensitive communication" to better understand the role of the senses in our perception of the world and interaction with other beings. His most recent book Strategic Communication and Deformative Transparency. Persuasion in politics, propaganda and public health (Routledge) explores the representations of the grotesque in public communication. He was director of the healthcare practice for Latin America at Burson-Marsteller.

Davide Nicolini is Professor of Organization Studies at Warwick Business School (UK) where he co-directs the IKON Research Centre and coordinates the Practice, Process and Institution Research Program. His current research focuses on the development of the practice-based approach and the refinement and promotion of processual, relational and materialist research methods.

Linda Rouleau is professor at the management department of HEC Montreal (Canada). She is co-responsible for the GéPS (Study Group of strategy-as-practice, HEC Montreal). Her research work focuses on the practice of strategy in pluralistic contexts, middle managers sense-making and organizational issues in extreme contexts. In the last few years, she has published in peer-reviewed journals such as *Academy of Management Review*, *Organization Science*, *Accounting*, *Organization and Society*, *Journal of Management Studies*, *Human Relations*, etc. She is co-responsible for the GéPS (Study Group of strategy-as-practice, HEC Montreal). She is senior editor at Organization Studies and member of the editorial team of Organizational Research Methods.

Viviane Sergi is Associate Professor in the Department of Management at UQAM School of Management in Montréal, Canada. Her research interests include process thinking, performativity, the transformation of work, leadership, and materiality. Her recent studies have explored how communication is, in various settings, constitutive of organizational phenomena, such as new work practices, strategy and leadership. She also has a keen interest for methodological issues related to qualitative research and for the practice of academic writing. Her work has been published in journals such as *Academy of Management Annals*, *Human Relations*, *Scandinavian Journal of Management*, *Long Range Planning*, *Management* and in *Qualitative Research in Organizations and Management*.

Elizabeth Wilhoit Larson is assistant professor in the School of Communication and Journalism at Auburn University (US). She is an organizational communication scholar whose research focuses on materiality in organizations, organizationality, and gendered careers.

List of Figures

List of Tables

CHAPTER 1

Introduction

Sylvie Grosjean and Frédérik Matte

Abstract This introduction presents a short review of existing video-based research in organizations by highlighting how these researches address the material, embodied, and sensorial dimensions of the workplace practices. We then introduce the purpose of the book and present the three main sections: (1) video-ethnography and reflexivity-in-practice: making visible the embodied and sensory dimensions of work practices, (2) video-ethnography and organizing spaces: sensing places and the multiple nature of working spaces, and (3) "outsider" and "insider" video-ethnographer: exploring multimodal and multisensorial workplace settings.

Keywords Video-based research · Organizations · Workplace practices · Multimodal · Sensory

S. Grosjean (✉) · F. Matte
University of Ottawa, Ottawa, ON, Canada
e-mail: sylvie.grosjean@uottawa.ca

F. Matte
e-mail: fmatt3@uottawa.ca

S. Grosjean and F. Matte (eds.), *Organizational Video-Ethnography Revisited*, https://doi.org/10.1007/978-3-030-65551-8_1

1.1 Video-Based Research in Organizations

Various forms of organizational video-ethnography have been used over the years for studying organizational life (e.g., Cooren et al. 2008; Smets et al. 2014; LeBaron et al. 2018; Hassard et al. 2018). Researchers (see Llewellyn and Hindmarsh 2010; Heath and Luff 2018; Christianson 2018) emphasize the materiality and embodiment in everyday interaction using video to capture and analyze the workplace practices. For example, Samra-Fredericks studied "everyday strategic management practice-as-interactionally-done" (2010: 198). Liu and Maitlis (2014) also examined the relationships between emotions and strategy by capturing and analyzing the multimodal nature of strategy-in-practice (e.g., body movements, facial expressions). Video-ethnography thus explores the ways individuals accomplish practical activities in and through interaction with others and with a variety of resources such as texts, bodies, tools, technologies, objects, and so on (e.g. Fele 2012; Balogun et al. 2014; Skjælaaen et al. 2020). In sum, this type of research is mobilized to "*zoom in*" on the social interactions, "*zoom out*" to understand the context in which these interactions occur and also used to "*zoom with*" to better appreciate the participants' perspectives (Nicolini 2009; Jarrett and Liu 2018).

Furthermore, recent studies involving the senses, bodies, and materiality have expanded their scope of inquiry by integrating dimensions of work practices that cannot always be clearly verbalized or identified (Paterson and Glass 2018; Hassard et al. 2018). This is notably the case with the multisensoriality of experience and emotions (Gherardi 2017; Mondada 2019; Gibson and Vom Lehn 2020; Grosjean et al. 2020). In numerous organizational contexts, workers use their body and senses to guide their everyday activities (Yakhlef 2010; Paterson and Glass 2018). Research indeed reveals how clinicians, architects, or other professionals rely on "sensible knowledge" to orient their practice (Strati 2007). The researchers' role is thus to explore the many ways in which the embodied and sensitive nature of organizational knowledge is at play. As Gherardi (2019) shows:

> technologies such as video recording, photo-voice, and mobile digital technologies for real-time ethnography are expanding the possibilities to record and analyze the entire range of what Toraldo et al. (2016) have called

> 'elusive knowledges' comprising tacit, aesthetic, and embodied aspects of organizational life that are difficult to articulate. (p. 747)

Video-ethnography allows researchers to apprehend organizations and workplace settings multi-modally and multi-sensorially and contribute to conduct thick description and analysis of organizational phenomena (Vannini 2017). In this context, multimodal analysis is increasing in popularity because it allows researchers to study workplace practices as activities located, organized and interactionally based on a variety of processes such as speech, gestures, body movements, and object manipulations (Streeck et al. 2011). In fact, organizational activities are embedded in a complex entanglement of people, documents, computers, and instruments and it is therefore important to understand how these various artifacts are assembled, interpreted, negotiated, and translated in the course of actions in order to understand the role they play in the interaction. For various researchers (Raulet-Croset and Borzeix 2014; Harris 2016; Pink 2008, 2015; Groot Kormelink and Costera Meijer 2019; Gherardi 2019), video recording is recognized for its capacity to capture embodied movements or gestures, to follow sensory practices or to apprehend affective atmospheres of places. In other words, to record the multimodality and multisensoriality of communication processes can 'facilitate an appreciation of the practical, sensual and affective dimensions' (Brown and Banks 2015: 98) of the organizational world. As mentioned by Vannini (2017):

> video methods are absolutely essential tools in the research toolkit of ethnographers. Video methods' more-than-representational multimodality can allow us to cultivate the meaningfulness of our visual and aural engagement with the world and hone the esthetic evocativeness of our strategies of knowledge generation. (p. 162)

With the growing interest in sociomateriality (e.g., Orlikowski and Scott 2008; Leonardi 2012; Hindmarsh and Llewellyn 2018) and the development of research on the embodied and sensory dimensions of organizational practices, we argue that the methodological challenges of this type of research need to be addressed more thoroughly. We also need to reflect on how it can be done with video recording as a primary method. As mentioned by Hassard et al. (2018):

> to advance new conceptual logic for video-based organizational research, we supplant the objectivist and realist philosophy underpinning traditional documentary filmmaking with sociologically interpretive and reflexive arguments for undertaking ethnography in organizations, a subjective process which importantly yields greater understanding of affect and embodiment. (p. 1403)

This book intends to address this issue by exploring the undeveloped potential of video-ethnography to study the material, emotional and sensory dimensions of workplace practices. Researchers in organizational studies need to better recognize this type of ethnographic methods and we do so by revisiting various forms of organizational video-ethnography that make organizational phenomena visible and help better appreciate the organizing properties of bodies, affects, senses, and spaces in workplace practices.

1.2 Studying the Material, Embodied, and Sensory Practices in Organizations

The main purpose of the book is to bring forth a new analytic glance at bodies, materiality and senses in organization through video-ethnographies that document professional practices and organizational spaces. In other words, the book offers various methodological approaches to explore and analyze in micro-detail the manifestations of embodied and sensory dimensions of organizational life. To do so, we have divided the book into three sections: (1) video-ethnography and reflexivity-in-practice: making visible the embodied and sensory dimensions of work practices, (2) video-ethnography and organizing spaces: sensing places and the multiple nature of working spaces, and (3) "outsider" and "insider" video-ethnographer: exploring multimodal and multisensorial workplace settings.

Firstly, we discuss how video recordings provide the basis for a more reflexive understanding of organizational phenomenon. Video recordings are used by researchers to stimulate a reflective process that explicitly solicits the participants' interpretations of their video-recorded interactions. This methodological apparatus underlines the added value of video reflexivity to study affects and senses in workplace practices. More so, the methodological focus contributes to the understanding of the way bodies, senses, and affects in organizations are constitutive of workplace practices (e.g., clinical decision-making, medical radiology, telemedicine). The authors of this book have designed their methods by using video recordings not only to propose a fine-grained analysis of behaviors, actions, or learning processes in organization but by being aware that we must remain conscious of what the camera does not let us see.

The chapter written by Rick Iedema and Jeff Bezemer sets out the premises, practices, and achievements of video-reflexive ethnography or VRE. VRE focuses on engendering an affective, deliberative, and pragmatic dynamic among its participants by visually representing and negotiating both mundane and complex facets of care processes in which participants are involved. This makes VRE a uniquely participative and appreciative endeavor: rather than researcher-analysts deciding what are the critical analytical categories and procedures, and what are the most significant findings and conclusions, VRE invites and encourages participants (professionals, patients, families, and so on) to articulate their responses to footage portraying their own and their colleagues' work practices and circumstances. The authors describe how reflexive meetings enable participants to respond to each other's views, responses, and suggestions. Participants thus come to realize and contextualize what are their own, what are others', and what are not-yet-considered perspectives on the work and work contexts depicted. The chapter presents case study examples to illustrate VRE's philosophy which aims not to reconstruct the real from knowledge about the past, but to construct futures from collaborative learning about the present.

Laurent Filliettaz proposes a reflection on the specific instructional practices that emerge when newcomers in medical radiology gain access to such technical skills in the conditions of practice, under the guidance of experienced workers endorsing the role of mentors. When learning to become technicians in radiology, students are faced with a wide scope of technical objects, including X-ray devices, scanners, or RMI technology. They also have to learn how to position the patient's body so that adequate images are produced for diagnostic or therapeutic purposes. Laurent Filliettaz tries to understand how participants in interactions—including students, mentors, and patients—use material resources to accomplish complex and layered actions, oriented simultaneously or alternatively to the production of work and knowledge associated with work. More specifically, this chapter aims at understanding how participants may use the patient's body as resources to navigate complex constraints associated with work procedures and epistemic practices. To do so, Laurent Filliettaz adopts the theoretical perspective of multimodal interaction analysis and uses a collection of audio-video data recorded in a public hospital of the canton of Geneva in Switzerland.

Sylvie Grosjean, Frédérik Matte, and Isaac Nahon-Serfaty explore how video reflexivity is used to study the ways in which sensory information is changed and redistributed by the use of telemedicine technologies. As mentioned by Maslen (2017), they also make visible the ways in which sensory work in the context of telemedicine is a methodological challenge. In this chapter, the authors address this challenge with a methodological approach based on the two-sides of video-ethnography. They present a methodological apparatus based on the video recordings of situated clinical activities in telemedicine (video-ethnography called the "bright side") and video self-confrontation with physicians (called the "hidden side"). This methodological approach aims to produce an interpretative framework of clinical practice in telemedicine by the doctors themselves to make visible various forms of "sensing-at-distance."

Secondly, different usages of video-ethnography inform our understanding of organizational spaces and places (Laurier 2004). There is a growing attention to spaces and places in organization studies, particularly in the context of more flexible, collaborative, and mobile work arrangements as coworking spaces, or due to the recent material turn in organization studies (de Vaujany and Mitev 2013; Meunier and Vásquez 2008; Mengis et al. 2018). Video shadowing or participant viewpoint ethnography (PVE), opens a window on the various ways to make sense of organization spaces or mobile working spaces (e.g., how organizing practices take place in mobile situations). The methodological apparatus presented in this section contributes to our understanding of organizational spaces as progressively constituted by the entanglement of the embodied, material, and sensory dimensions of organizing. Organizations or mobile working spaces are not only spaces of work but places where people engage through their material, sensory, and embodied practices in an "ongoing reordering" of these spaces (Mengis et al. 2018).

Jeanne Mengis and Davide Nicolini discuss, in their chapter, how diffractive methodologies can enrich visual and video-based research methods. Diffraction is a term derived from physics. It refers to a particular kind of interference whereby waves overlap to generate new patterns. In human and social science research, diffractive methodologies aim to expand the understanding of objects of study by creating generative interferences and differences. This chapter illustrates three ways of practicing diffraction in visual and video research including (1) reading texts intra-actively; (2) reading the performing of an apparatus through another; (3) creating interactions among different forms of participation in interventionist research. The authors suggest that by multiplying our sociotechnical and relational ways of conducting video research and by reading one video-methodological engagement through the other, diffractive methodologies help us generate inventive provocations and produce new meanings.

In his chapter, Nicolas Bencherki asks the following question: Why are visual methods, and in particular video methods, so naturally associated with the study of space in organizational studies? This chapter suggests that both videos and space having been shown to be *relational* phenomena. By combining work in relational studies of space with French philosopher Gilles Deleuze's writings on moving images, the author formulates a communicative approach to the analysis of space using video data. Nicolas Bencherki proposes three sets of relationalities that reflexively fold into one another: (1) the spatial relations more or less faithfully represented in the data; (2) the relations that are outside the data but that made it possible; and (3) the relations defining the observation context. Through actual video shadowing data, he illustrates that accounting for all three sets of relationalities provides a more complete understanding of what goes on in and around the space, not omitting participants' and researchers' embodied experience of it.

Finally, Elizabeth Wilhoit Larson describes a specific video research method called: participant viewpoint ethnography (PVE) that involves two components. First, a participant uses a wearable camera to create a video from their perspective of some activity. Second, the researcher watches the video with the participant and interviews them about the video. This method is useful to help participants attend to aspects of their experience that may be innate and difficult to verbalize and gives the researcher better understanding of the embodied aspects of activities. It is illustrated with an example from the author's research on bike commuters. Finally, Elizabeth Wilhoit Larson proposes future research directions for using PVE to study mobilities in organizations are suggested.

The last section presents studies that analyze, via video recordings of daily activities (inside and outside organizations), how strategies or emotions are constituted through interactions in real-time. In numerous organizational contexts, workers use their bodies and their senses as guides, in the conduct of their everyday activity and video-ethnography is a useful device to grasp multi-situated interactions (e.g., during formal or informal meetings). In addition, and to conclude our reflection on video-ethnography, this section addresses how complementary data produced via social media could complement the analysis of work activities.

The chapter written by Feng Liu, Michael Jarrett, and Linda Rouleau draws on their own journeys and on other studies to search for and develop appropriate methods to study top management team strategic decision-making in real-time meetings. After introducing video-based approaches in organizational research, the chapter proposes three ways of including research participants' perspectives in our interpretations to close the gap between "insider" and "outsider" views of the research process and outcomes. The authors call these methodological approaches: refining, distributive, and holistic. They are presented and evaluated based on selected video episodes from the authors' and other studies.

In the last chapter, Viviane Sergi and Claudine Bonneau argue that paying attention to the mundane aspects of work enriches our understanding of individuals' lived experience in organizations. While capturing these mundane aspects can be carried through video-ethnography, the authors propose that mundane data found on social media might also lead to such an investigation. Using examples from their previous work, Viviane Sergi and Claudine Bonneau explore how mundane data found on social media can reveal dimensions of work practices. They also show that it can offer a valuable contribution to video-ethnographic methods in three ways. First, it can feed in situ video-ethnographic data collection, by providing complimentary data on dimensions that are already explored through a video-ethnographic approach. Second, social media can broaden the research site by allowing video-ethnographers to extend their presence and pursue their work through different channels, temporalities, and places. Finally, it allows researchers to access and document important dimensions of work practices, including aesthetic, affective and embodied facets of work and other experiences, that would otherwise be difficult to capture through video-ethnography.

References

Balogun, J., Jacobs, C., Jarzabkowski, P., Mantere, S., & Vaara, E. (2014). Placing strategy discourse in context: Sociomateriality, sensemaking, and power. *Journal of Management Studies, 51*(2), 175–201.

Brown, K., & Banks, E. (2015). Close encounters: Using mobile video ethnography to understand human–animal relations. In C. Bates (Ed.), *Video methods: Social science research in motion* (pp. 95–120). London: Routledge.

Christianson, M. K. (2018). Mapping the terrain: The use of video-based research in top-tier organizational journals. *Organizational Research Methods, 21*(2), 261–287.

Cooren, F., Brummans, B. H. J. M., & Charrieras, D. (2008). The coproduction of organizational presence: A Study of Médecins sans Frontières in action. *Human Relations, 61,* 1339–1370.

de Vaujany, F.-X., & Mitev, N. (2013). *Materiality and space: Organizations, artefacts and practices*. Palgrave Macmillan.

Fele, G. (2012). The use of video to document tacit participation in an emergency operations centre. *Qualitative Research, 12*(3), 280–303.

Gherardi, S. (2017). One turn… and now another one: Do the turn to practice and the turn to affect have something in common? *Management Learning, 48*(3), 345–358.

Gherardi, S. (2019). Theorizing affective ethnography for organization studies. *Organization, 26*(6), 741–760.

Gibson, W., & Vom Lehn, D. (2020). Seeing as accountable action: The interactional accomplishment of sensorial work. *Current Sociology, 68*(1), 77–96.

Groot Kormelink, T., & Costera Meijer, I. (2019). Material and sensory dimensions of everyday news use. *Media, Culture and Society, 41*(5), 637–653.

Grosjean, S., Matte, F., & Nahon-Serfaty, I. (2020). "Sensory Ordering" in Nurses' Clinical Decision-Making: Making Visible Senses, Sensing and "Sensory Work" in the Hospital. *Symbolic Interaction, Special Issue "The Senses in Interaction"*. https://doi.org/10.1002/symb.490.

Harris, A. (2016). *Video as Method*. Oxford University Press.

Hassard, J., Burns, D., Hyde, P., & Burns, J. P. (2018). A visual turn for organizational ethnography: Embodying the subject in video-based research. *Organization Studies, 39*(10), 1403–1424.

Heath, C., & Luff, P. (2018). The naturalistic experiment: Video and organizational interaction. *Organizational Research Methods, 21*(2), 466–488.

Hindmarsh, J., & Llewellyn, N. (2018). Video in sociomaterial investigations: A solution to the problem of relevance for organizational research. *Organizational Research Methods, 21*(2), 412–437.

Jarrett, M., & Liu, F. (2018). "Zooming with": A participatory approach to video ethnography in organizational studies. *Organizational Research Methods, 21*, 366–385.

Laurier, E. (2004). Doing office work on the motorway. *Theory, Culture & Society, 21*, 261–277.

LeBaron, C., Jarzabkowski, P., Pratt, M. G., & Fetzer, G. (2018). An introduction to video methods. *Organizational Research, 21*(2), 239–260.

Leonardi, P. M. (2012). Materiality, sociomateriality, and socio-technical systems: What do these terms mean? How are they different? Do we need them? In P. M. Leonardi, B. A. Nardi, & J. Kallinikos (Eds.), *Materiality and organizing: Social interaction in a technological world* (pp. 25–48). Oxford University Press.

Liu, F., & Maitlis, S. (2014). Emotional dynamics and strategizing processes: A study of strategic conversations in top team meetings. *Journal of Management Studies, 51*(2), 202–234.

Llewellyn, N., & Hindmarsh, J. (Eds.). (2010). *Organisation, interaction and practice: Studies of ethnomethodology and conversation analysis*. Cambridge University Press.

Maslen, S. (2017). Layers of sense: The sensory work of diagnostic sensemaking in digital health. *Digital Health, 3*, 2055207617709101.

Mengis, J., Nicolini, D., & Gorli, M. (2018). The video production of space: How different recording practices matter. *Organizational Research Methods, 21*(2), 288–315.

Meunier, D., & Vásquez, C. (2008). On Shadowing the hybrid character of actions: A communicational approach. *Communication Methods and Measures, 2*(3), 167–192.

Mondada, L. (2019). Contemporary issues in conversation analysis: Embodiment and materiality, multimodality and multisensoriality in social interaction. *Journal of Pragmatics, 145*, 47–62.

Nicolini, D. (2009). Zooming in and out: Studying practices by switching theoretical lenses and trailing connections. *Organization Studies, 30*(12), 1391–1418.

Orlikowski, W. J., & Scott, S. V. (2008). 10 sociomateriality: Challenging the separation of technology, work and organization. *Academy of Management Annals, 2*(1), 433–474.

Paterson, M., & Glass, M. R. (2018). Seeing, feeling, and showing 'bodies-in-place': Exploring reflexivity and the multisensory body through videography. *Social and Cultural Geography, 21*(1), 1–24.

Pink, S. (2008). An urban tour: The sensory sociality of ethnographic place-making. *Ethnography, 9*(2), 175–196.

Pink, S. (2015). *Doing Sensory Ethnography*. Sage.

Raulet-Croset, N., & Borzeix, A. (2014). Researching spatial practices through commentated walks: "On the move" and "walking with". *Journal of Organizational Ethnography, 3*(1), 27–42.
Samra-Fredericks, D. (2010). The interactional accomplishment of a strategic plan. In N. Llewellyn & J. Hindmarsh (Ed.), *Organisation, interaction and practice: Studies in ethnomethodology and conversation analysis* (pp. 198–217). Cambridge University Press.
Skjælaaen, G. R., Bygdås, A. L., & Hagen, A. L. (2020). Visual inquiry: Exploring embodied organizational practices by collaborative film-elicitation. *Journal of Management Inquiry, 29*(1), 59–75.
Smets, M., Burke, G., Jarzabkowski, P., & Spee, P. (2014). Charting new territory for organizational ethnography: Insights from a team-based video ethnography. *Journal of Organizational Ethnography, 3*(1), 10–26.
Strati, A. (2007). Sensible knowledge and practice-based learning. *Management Learning, 38*(1), 61–77.
Streeck, J., Goodwin, C., & LeBaron, L. (2011). *Embodied interaction, language and body in the material world*. Cambridge University Press.
Toraldo, M. L., Islam, G., & Mangia, G. (2016). Modes of knowing: Video research and the problem of elusive knowledges. *Organizational Research Methods, 21*(2), 438–465.
Vannini, P. (2017). Low and Slow: Notes on the production and distribution of a mobile video ethnography. *Mobilities, 12*(1), 155–166.
Yakhlef, A. (2010). The corporeality of practice-based learning. *Organization Studies, 31*(4), 409–430.

PART I

Video-Ethnography and Reflexivity-in-Practice: Making Visible the Embodied and Sensory Dimensions of Work Practices

CHAPTER 2

Video-Ethnography and Video-Reflexive Ethnography: Investigating and Expanding Learning About Complex Realities

Rick Iedema and Jeff Bezemer

Abstract The chapter provides an overview of both video-ethnography and video-reflexive ethnography. It relates these two orientations as providing complementary perspectives on socio-organizational complexity, and on enabling learning about that complexity. The first section provides background to the video-ethnographic and video-reflexive endeavours that have been published in the last decade or so. The second section provides two examples; one from the domain of gall bladder surgery, and one from ward-based infection control. The chapter's discussion offers some generalisations and delves into the links between visuality, complexity and pedagogy, before concluding with the

R. Iedema (✉)
King's College London, London, UK
e-mail: rick.iedema@kcl.ac.uk

J. Bezemer (✉)
University College London, London, UK
e-mail: j.bezemer@ucl.ac.uk

S. Grosjean and F. Matte (eds.), *Organizational Video-Ethnography Revisited*, https://doi.org/10.1007/978-3-030-65551-8_2

assertion that visualization will grow in scholarly significance given the rising emphasis in contemporary civilizations on increasingly attuned, more multimodal, and more flexible ways of seeing and doing.

Keywords Video-reflexive ethnography · Learning · Team · Healthcare · Visual methods · Multimodality

2.1 Introduction

Visual methodologies have gained in prominence in recent years thanks to the widening availability and portability of cameras, batteries and screen technologies, easier access to and use of editing software, and greater public acceptability of the visual medium for purposes other than formal information dissemination and social entertainment (Pink 2007). The rise in popularity of the visual medium in academic research also needs to be understood in the context of scholars' growing interest in complex phenomena—phenomena whose visualization adds affective, embodied, spatial and temporal dimensions to what otherwise might have to rely on the linear and monomodal means of linguistic description. Visuality offers more routes into and through complexity—a factor that no doubt explains much of its current popularity in contemporary scholarship focusing on fast-changing social and institutional domains and the wicked problems that define these domains (Iedema et al. 2013).

Visualization of in situ processes and practices enables scholars to engage with the multimodal dimensions of complex contexts and wicked problems (Goodwin and Goodwin 1998; Goodwin 1995). The fine-grained manifestation of the bodily movements, kinesics and proxemics that accompany, structure and enrich discursive interaction may highlight aspects of sociality that transcription risks omitting from the analysis (Knoblauch et al. 2006; Jewitt et al. 2016). In recent years, rich schemas have been developed for the production and analysis of video data, combining in-depth conversation analytical scholarship with expertise in bodily and spatial movement (Heath et al. 2010), linguistic analysis that nets in spatial, embodied and affective dynamics (Bezemer 2020; Thibault 2011), and anthropological ethnography that nets in the visual-temporal dimensions of in situ sociality (Redmon 2019).

In addition to the rise in visual-analytical scholarship, there is now increasing interest also in participatory visual methods (Milne et al. 2012). To date, statements of participatory principle and interventionist intent (Hassard et al. 2018; Bauman et al. 2019) still outnumber actual instantiations and local realizations of participatory visual scholarship (Iedema et al. 2013). The difficulty of putting participatory visual scholarship into practice notwithstanding, these approaches' democratic and experimental ethos does not stop at handing the analytical reins back to those represented in the visuals and the footage. Rather, this ethos extends to inviting participants to be party to decision-making about what to video, how to video, what to edit, what to show back to participants, what to say about the footage, what learning and conclusions to draw from what is shown and discussed, and what then to integrate into relationships, practices and systems (Iedema et al. 2006).

To do justice to these two recent developments in visual enquiry, the present chapter provides an overview of both video-ethnography and video-reflexive ethnography. The chapter relates these two orientations as providing complementary perspectives on socio-organizational complexity, and on enabling learning about that complexity. The chapter is structured as follows: the next section provides more background to video ethnographic and video-reflexive endeavours that have been published in the last decade or so. The section after that provides two examples; one from the domain of gall bladder surgery, and one from ward-based infection control. The chapter's discussion delves more deeply into the links between visuality, complexity and pedagogy, before concluding with the assertion that visualization will only grow in scholarly significance given the rising emphasis in contemporary civilizations on increasingly attuned, more multimodal, and more flexible ways of seeing and doing.

2.2 Background: Video-Ethnography and Video-Reflexive Ethnography

Video-ethnography involves the visualization for ethnographic purposes of social and organizational processes and dynamics. Here, 'for ethnographic purposes' means that video-editing conventions are not imposed to create, sustain or enhance a particular narrative or argument. On the contrary, ethnographic video will seek to privilege an original or 'natural' continuity of process or event in real-time, thus respecting the spatio-temporal integrity of social-organizational phenomena, as well as the messy and complex aspects of events as they unfold. Video-ethnography thus targets and captures socio-organizational happenings as they may be experienced and witnessed by someone (i.e. the camera person) dispassionately and from a relative distance: 'video ethnography is a cinematic approach to recording ethnographic expressions of lived experiences' (Redmon 2019: 3).

As approach, video-ethnography (VE) now provides a meeting place for documentary makers (Redmon 2019; Rouch 2003), anthropologists (Pink 2007), cultural geographers (Rose 2016), sociologists (Heath and Hindmarsh 2002), semioticians and discourse analysts (Bezemer et al. 2011), psychologists and therapists (James et al. 2015) and organizational theorists (Iedema et al. 2013), each investing VE with their own unique political, methodological and analytical priorities to the use and analysis of video data. What unites these scholars, no doubt, is what Redmon identifies as VE's capacity to 'plunge [us] into lived experience' and capture its multimodal manifestation:

> Video ethnography plunges into lived experience and offers a bodily, visual, and sonic mode of evocation of subjects and their worlds, expanding the available means of knowledge production beyond the written text or written description. (Redmon 2019: 3)

VE takes us well beyond conventional textual renderings of sociality, making possible engagement with facets of behaviour and interaction that transcription is hard pushed to reproduce: the embodied, affective, sub-conscious (prepersonal), and systemic (transpersonal) dimensions of everyday life. At the same time, the self-evident appearance of the imagery or footage is called into question through the need to make decisions about camera distance and focus, angle, duration, inclusions/exclusions, and so forth. These matters all concern decisions that foreground the role of those wielding the camera, and undo any claims about representational realism (Vannini 2015).

Further, VE provides opportunities for a variety of disciplinary angles on moving-image content. In this chapter therefore, one of our tasks is to focus on the depth of vision and insight that becomes possible through the visualization and in-depth analysis of events that otherwise might escape our attention. Consider in this regard how Heath and colleagues describe the intricate detail of an operating theatre interaction:

> ... how the instrument or material is passed to the surgeon is prospectively oriented to the specifics of the particular action that will be undertaken on this occasion. The way in which a particular object is passed enables the surgeon to grasp and apply the instrument or material without the necessity to adjust or reposition the way in which it is received and held. The character of these exchanges suggests an extraordinary economy of action that relies on the ability of the scrub nurse to prospectively envisage just how the instrument or material will be deployed on this occasion and pass the object to enable the relevant grasping that in turn eases its application. (Heath et al. 2018: 303)

Complementing this fine-grained video-analytical approach, video-reflexive ethnography moves the research focus from in-depth analysis of available video data to the collaborative construction of a practical question (or questions) to be addressed by participants and researchers; negotiation over what kinds of visual data may be gathered (and how) to help them answer this question (or questions), and shared reflection using footage of participants' own circumstances, spaces, relations and practices (Iedema et al. 2013, 2019, 2006).

Video-reflexive ethnography (VRE) compensates as it were for the 'representational realism' that inevitably and necessarily motivates VE to enable it to concentrate on moving-image content and to make ontological claims about in situ practice and human sociality (Vannini 2015). VRE diverges from VE's focus on content and its concern with ontological claims by shifting VRE's point of gravity to the relationships that obtain between researchers and participants (Iedema and Carroll 2015). This shift is explained with reference to VRE's ultimate goal: to engage participants (and not just researchers) in learning about the circumstances, spaces, relations and practices in which they are embroiled. VRE's main inspirations include Rouch's (2003) and MacDougall's (2006) participatory approaches to video-making, Wittgenstein's (1953) meaning-making games, post-cognitivist developments in social psychology (Still and Costall 1991) including Shotter's (1993) account of 'conversational realities', and Engeström's Vygotskyan theory and video-enabled methodology underpinning 'expansive learning' (Engeström 2008).

In essence, and in contrast to VE's micrological and analytical revelations, VRE is a potentiation technology (Andersen and Stenner 2019); a technology that expands participants' capacities for being and acting. Potentiation refers to learning that reaches into the affective, embodied and habituated dimensions of people's lives. A potentiation technology is a means that confronts participants with aspects of their own ways of being, saying, feeling and doing, and which they have come to take for granted to the point of having learned to forget these. The potentiation process creates 'liminality' (Stenner 2018): that is, a space outside of habituation and familiarity where participants' relationship to themselves, others and the world is questioned and potentially altered. Potentiation thus means that participants are enabled through finding themselves at the liminal edges of their taken-as-given life to ask questions about and experiment with their and others' ways of being, saying, feeling and doing. To achieve a safe environment in which such potentiating learning can occur, VRE researchers' primary concern is to build a 'weave of commitment' among participants (Iedema et al. 2013) which will sustain them when confronted with the (at times sub-ideal) realities of their ways of being, thinking, saying, feeling and doing (Iedema 2020).

Examples of VRE studies are ones that have involved patients at the end of their lives reflecting on their dying trajectories (Collier et al. 2016), patients reflecting on clinicians' infection control methods (Wyer et al. 2017), clinicians' re-evaluating their approach to breast milk sharing (Carroll 2014), ambulance paramedics and emergency clinicians in developing a programme of communication to ensure the safety, appropriateness and comprehensiveness of their handovers (Iedema et al. 2012), to name but some (see Iedema et al. 2013, 2019: for more examples).

In what follows, we describe two case studies that focus on complex care circumstances. Both studies used video to capture care complexity, but they did so in different ways. Using an 'outside' perspective, the first study captured and analysed a surgical trainee being guided through a complex surgical procedure. Here, the focus of attention is on the trainee's surgical moves, and the commentary this attracts from him and the senior consultant monitoring these moves. Adopting an 'inside' perspective, the second study visualized for a team of clinicians their own infection control efforts, and analysed the space that this feedback process created for team-internal deliberation and reflection. We provide these accounts not just to explore the nature of in situ behaviour amidst complexity, but also to highlight VE-VRE complementarity, and then to outline the methodological and theoretical connections among visuality, complexity, reflexivity and learning.

2.3 Two Video-Based Studies

The two studies described here both focused on the moment-to-moment unfolding of care. The first was a video-ethnographic programme of work targeting clinical practice in the operating theatres of a major teaching hospital in London (Bezemer et al. 2019). The sequence focused on here is taken from a collection of 14 video-recorded laparoscopic cholecystectomy cases, involving 6 consultant surgeons and 6 surgical trainees. In this sequence, a surgical trainee in his fourth year of specialty training ('ST4') is performing the operation under the supervision of a consultant. The consultant is not 'scrubbed in' (and therefore is not able to intervene); he watches the operation on one of the screens in theatre projecting the laparoscopic view.

The second study involved clinicians and patients in video-reflexive ethnography whose central component is frontline actors' reviewing footage of their infection control behaviour as they provide (or receive) care. This study took place in two Sydney metropolitan teaching hospitals with a total of 177 participants: 107 nurses, 44 doctors, 9 allied health staff, and 17 administrative or cleaning staff (Gilbert et al. 2020; Hooker et al. 2020; Iedema et al. 2018). It took place over 3 months in the ICU of one hospital and in two mixed surgical wards in a second hospital. Eighteen reflexive sessions were conducted in total. Prior to, as well as during, the video-reflexive ethnography, ward observations and interviews were carried out.

2.3.1 *'I Think You're Fine There'*

Our first description portrays surgeons at work, engaging in a routine elective operation: the laparoscopic cholecystectomy. In the UK, this procedure is performed more than 60,000 times each year (National Institute for Health and Care Excellence 2014). The study aim was to explore how surgeons define, recognize and respond to challenges in the context of this procedure, and how they enhance their capacity in this regard. The stills in Fig. 2.1 and the accompanying transcript give an impression of how the operation unfolded. The transcript captures the 'run up' to what surgeons generally recognize as a complex manoeuvre, namely the dividing of the cystic duct and the cystic artery.

Some background is needed to appreciate the challenges inherent in this surgical manoeuvre. After the introduction of laparoscopic cholecystectomy in the 1990s reports were published showing a notable increase

I think you're fine there

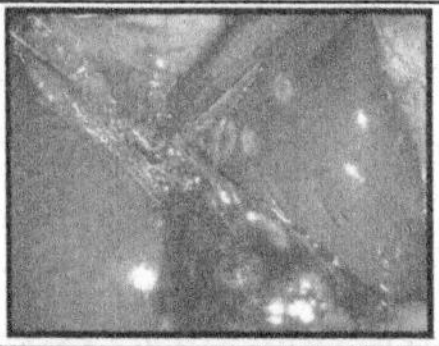	*Enters the space between cystic duct and cystic artery* Cons: I think you're fine there now M. I'd jus I'd just take it all
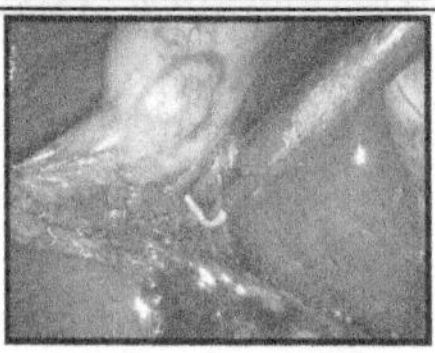	*Abandons space, pulls gall bladder down towards the liver* ST4: Clip em? Cons: Yeah.
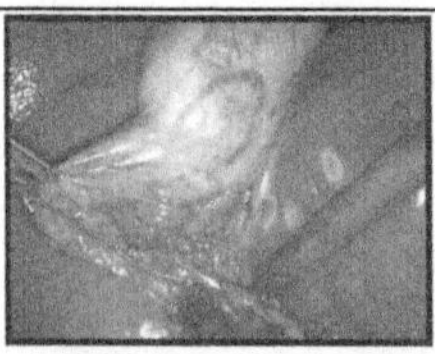	*Pushes stuff down* Cons: because you can see- if you just push up on the gall bladder- with your hook- just push up on the gall bladder - go through there
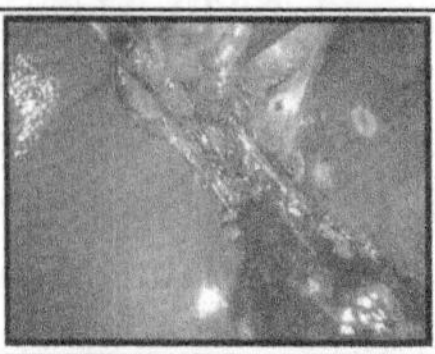	*Abandons space, now placing hook under gall bladder and pushing it up* Cons: and you can see you've got a nice big window there
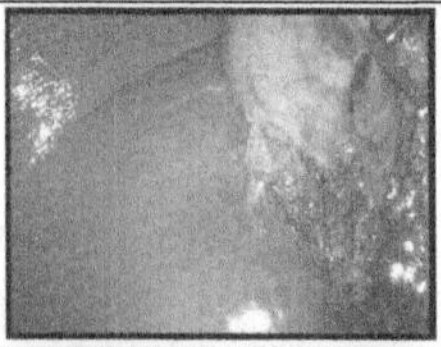	*Flips gall bladder over to expose other side* Cons: I mean the ideal is you take all that stuff and you make a big window but
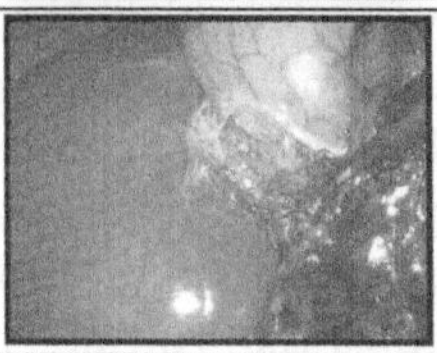	*Gently applies hook to bottom left structure*

Fig. 2.1 Extract and visual from a laparoscopic cholecystectomy (Cons = consultant surgeon, ST4 = surgical trainee in his fourth year of specialty training)

	*Flips back and places hook under gall bladder* ST4: Do you think I'm gonna have to take it from this side? Cons: Yeah. Well, I think you're fine
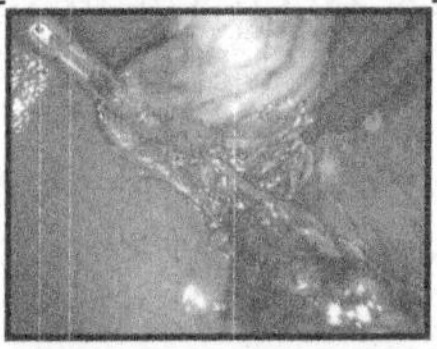	*Hooks up tissue, applies diathermy* Cons: There's something in there isn't there
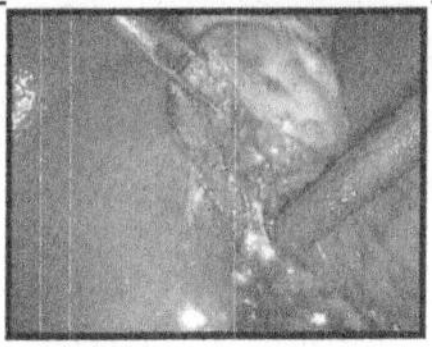	*Let's go of tissue, pulls up cystic artery and sweeps behind it* Cons: So you need to stay high on the gall bladder. So I'd take these structures ST4: Okay. Clips Cons: Take them around the gall bladder and you'll be fine ST4: Clips please

Fig. 2.1 (continued)

in cases where the cystic structures were misidentified, leading to injury of the common bile duct (a serious 'complication'). One of the responses to this increase has been the explication and teaching of identification methods, such as the 'Critical View of Safety' (CVS). This method involves checking, during a 'time-out' just before the cystic structures are divided, (1) that the surgeon has detached the lower part of the gall bladder from the liver; (2) that the surgeon has established that only two structures are attached to the gall bladder, and (3) that the surgeon has freed these structures from fatty and fibrous tissue (Strasberg and Brunt 2017). A range of other methods for systematically identifying the cystic structures have been described; there is as yet no official guideline however advocating one particular method.

During the operation in question here, surgeons 'slowed down' (Moulton et al. 2010) and examined the state of the cystic structures prior to dividing them. This involved exposing particular parts of the structures (e.g. by flipping them to one side) and viewing them from different angles; and 'touching' the structures with the tip of an instrument, drawing out their contours, and 'feeling' what is inside and around them. Through these examinations, visible to those co-present in the room in the moving image produced by the laparoscopic camera, they jointly engaged with the case 'in hand'.

The examinations were typically (in 13/14 cases) accompanied by verbal communication between consultant and trainee, in which they extrapolated beyond the case in hand. For example:

> That's what you call the critical view. Because now, I think here's the vessel. Well I can't do it more. So um can you (.) please that's what I want in all the cases. Is that okay? Here this is definitely going to the gall bladder and is not a continuous x of the cystic duct. (Consultant Surgeon)

With these verbal comments, consultants connected the personal ('I') to the collective ('you'), the momentary ('now') to the timeless ('always'), and token (identified by pointing) to type ('artery', 'cystic duct'). In this way, specific, momentary anatomical configurations were objectified ('that's the critical view') and courses of action in the here-and-now were validated ('therefore I can now divide the structures'). This validation occurred with reference to rules or principles that are claimed to have validity beyond the messiness of the here and now. Indeed, these rules/principles are terminologically and conceptually related to the published guidance referred to above; they represent common, consensual, professional knowledge.

It is important to note that these rules and principles in themselves cannot identify or generate best-for-now responses to local, emergent situations and complex problems. As instructions for (future) action they are of limited value to trainees. At the same time, the consultant's verbal guidance alone could not spell out what 'clean' or a 'nice big window' might mean. It is only the live image of in situ surgical experience that showed concrete instances of 'nice big windows' and other surgical categories. Coming about in the flux of the here-and-now, the knowing-cum-seeing that occurred during the operation became the actual ground for the consultants' situated actions and proposals for action: this unique confluence of knowing and experiencing drew the trainee's attention to the relevant anatomical specificities that were visible and to what was uniquely doable at this particular moment in time.

The limited generative or practical value of the general rules formulated by consultants is illustrated in the following episode highlighting a seemingly arbitrary and sudden decision (Fig. 2.1). Here, a trainee is operating, clearing the cystic structures, when the supervising consultant proposes to 'take it all'. In response, the trainee ceases his work on the structures and checks his understanding of this proposal ('Clip em?'), to which the consultant responds positively. It is noteworthy that in all but one of the 14 cases we observed did a consultant make this kind of unanticipated (by the trainee) call.

In the exchange that follows, the consultant sought to validate his proposal. He did this by getting the trainee to manipulate structures so as to create a particular view on the situation, and, when that view was obtained, by declaring that 'you've got a nice big window', thus explicating his interpretation of the current state of the structures being mobilized. He then contrasted the window in this patient to 'the ideal', intimating that at this point more dissection could certainly be done to add certainty. Nevertheless, the consultant stated, 'you're fine', and he did so twice, prompting the trainee to proceed to divide the structures.

The consultant also specified where the structures should be divided, namely high on the gall bladder, as 'there's something in there' (possibly referring to gall stones in the cystic duct). By drawing attention to this specific circumstance, he justified his proposal to deviate from 'the ideal' (more dissection) and divide the structures now ('So I'd take these structures'). His concern might have been that continued dissection could have caused damage and leaks (of gall and stones from the duct and blood from the artery). The decision to divide the structures, then, was not one that was fully evident, free of risk, and guaranteed of success. The learning that transpired for the trainee was that a common surgical procedure such as this may be complex and risky and can involve a trade-off between relative uncertainty and potential damage resulting from continued inspection. In short, this procedure's particular trajectory could not have been anticipated or captured by the explicit rules, principles and knowledge that are available to guide surgeons.

In summary, the consultant helped the surgical trainee appreciate the specifics of the situation, and connect these to more general considerations that applied to what he was seeing. The consultant talked the trainee through the procedure by highlighting identifiable anatomical features, attuning the trainee to risks and risk trade-offs, and guiding him through appropriate or at least feasible actions. In essence, the consultant provided the trainee with what is at once a more detailed and a more detached view of what was in front of them and on their actions. In this bifurcated way, the consultant modelled a way of seeing that is critical to the negotiation of in situ complexity: he wove together for the trainee formal knowledge (details of the surgical procedure, anatomical structures, the 'critical view of safety'), situational observations and experiences, the flux of activities, assessments of risk, and best-for-now scenarios for going on. Once the structures were surgically divided in an irreversible way, this delicate and dynamic configuration of knowledge and practice culminated in the (in this case successful) clinical-surgical outcome of the procedure, as well as fleeing into a memory of what just transpired. The trainee's recollection of this delicate and temporal confluence of knowing, seeing and doing will (or should) enable him to perform similar procedures going in the future.

2.3.2 *'That's a Good Idea'*

Our second initiative captured what happened when frontline actors scrutinized video footage of their own in situ practices. Where in the previous section the consultant helped the trainee distance himself from and learn about the flux of the here-and-now while in the midst of a surgical operation, this section homes in on a team of nurses viewing their own actions and decisions post hoc as they were replayed on a video screen (Iedema et al. 2019).

The participating team had just witnessed footage of team members administering medications to MRSA-positive patients in isolation rooms. The focus of the feedback meeting at issue here was on clinicians' behaviour in and around patients' isolation rooms. Its purpose was to explore how infection risk is handled and how it might be dealt with around patients with MRSA(Methicillin-resistant Staphylococcus aureus). The extract in Table 2.1 is taken from a transcript generated from a reflexive feedback meeting held in June 2013. Figure 2.2 provides a visual impression of the meeting.

The transcript extract (Table 2.1) shows the clinicians discussing the problem of how to avoid cross-infection when caring for patients in isolation rooms. The conversation about gloves, sharps, hand cream and charts arose because the nurses were shown a video clip in which their use of

Table 2.1 Extract from video-reflexive meeting (NUM = Nurse Unit Manager; N1/5/7/8/11 = Nurses; CNE = Clinical Nurse Educator)

NUM:	Yeah, but why would you take your gloves off if you're still carrying a sharp?
N5:	Yeah, that's it.
NUM:	You want to protect yourself when you're carrying the sharp.
N11:	That is not going to protect you. It's still going to pierce you if...
NUM:	Yeah... it's still got to get through the gloves first. But where she put the... where she put the kidney dish was straight on top of the desk.
N8:	Yeah.
...	
CNE:	Maybe we need sharps containers in every room?
N7:	That's right, yeah.
N8:	Yeah.
N3:	Yeah, that's a good idea.
CNE:	You know what I mean? Prevent all these...
N1:	The thing is, she's just done her hand cream, so the hand cream you can... you know... it's safety, so you can just push it so... I don't think it's any danger. Do you know what I mean?
NUM:	Yeah, but then if you get rid of the sharp within the room then you can also get rid of the kidney dish at the same time, straight into the bin.
N8:	That's right and then the gloves as well.
N1:	That's right, yeah.
CNE:	It's just minimizing all these risks.
NUM:	But still the big thing there is that chart getting taken into... into the patient's room. You go... when you put the gloves on you touch the patient, touch the gloves...

those objects highlighted infection risks previously not noticed. In effect, the facilitator (pointing at the display screen in the accompanying photo; Fig. 2.2) and the video clip together played a role not unlike that of the consultant surgeon above where the focus was on how to divide anatomical structures.

Thus, here too the nurses' attention was on an unfolding of in situ circumstances including care decisions and activities, material objects, clean/dirty boundaries and infection risks. These circumstances became discussable through the nurses' viewing (and thereby becoming distanced from) what would otherwise remain taken-as-given aspects of practice shown in the video clip. As in the surgery scenario, the nurses' comments vacillated between articulating the messiness of the situation and invoking formal rules and systemic constraints governing infection control, such as

Fig. 2.2 Visual impression of video-reflexive meeting

the rule to wear gloves while handling sharps, and the general availability of sharps containers. The practical problem that the video clip helped foreground—not in the first instance for the researchers but for the clinicians themselves, since this was the latter's concern—centred on what to do with used sharps while needing to proceed with the care. The suggestion that every isolation room needs a sharps container served to contain the problem that had now become reflexively apparent for those responsible for infection control. The clinicians' conversation picked up on this, and sought to flesh out and render workable a more appropriate and practical gloving and sharps use policy. The clinicians' visually-enabled realisation and the nature of their discussion have now opened their practice and practical awareness up to a reflexivity that is capable of tackling complex problems, at once netting in the local and the systemic dimensions of practice.

2.4 Discussion

The case studies targeted two different but related modes of activity: in situ meaning-making (foregrounded in VE) and post hoc meaning-making (foregrounded in VRE). In the first case study portraying the gall-bladder surgery, clinical practice is analysed and is shown to involve attentive teaching, deep concentration and careful 'reflection-in-action' (Schön 1983). This reflection-in-action is co-performed between the consultant surgeon and the trainee to ensure no damage is done to anatomical structures. The formal analysis of the video data was conducted collaboratively by a linguistic-ethnographer and a surgeon (not the one filmed) (Bezemer 2015; Bezemer et al. 2019). The case study presented one aspect of how the surgeons' reflection-in-action unfolded, how learning became possible, and how they made sense of and shared information about what was happening, what the risks were, and what should and could be done next.

In the second case study of nurses' everyday infection control, clinical practice unfolded in rather more hurried and in relatively habituated fashion, offering less evidence of and opportunity for 'reflection-in-action'. This second case study therefore foregrounded 'reflection-on-action' as a mode of activity that involved these same (videoed) practitioners in post hoc deliberation about what happened in practice, and what this reflection now made practically, relationally and psychologically possible. Instead of seeking to derive principles about how to teach and learn risky procedures, the VRE study involved the practitioners themselves in engendering personal and team-based insights about their own ways of working, reasoning and relating. This process resulted in dishabituation through asking self-directed questions, practice change, and (as documented in other publications) a more reflexive attitude among practitioners towards in situ infection risks and infection control behaviours (Iedema et al. 2015). Table 2.2 summarizes these differences (both studies had been ethically approved and participants had provided appropriate consent).

2.5 Conclusion

The two case studies described above-provided examples of video-ethnographic and video-reflexive ethnographic studies. The accounts made possible through these two visual-ethnographic endeavours offer

Table 2.2 *In situ/Post hoc* meaning-making

	In situ meaning-making	*Post hoc meaning-making*
VE case study	• process: videoing of gall-bladder operation • participants: operating trainee, unscrubbed supervisor • conditions: small, stationary team in operating theatre, limited time but no urgency: opportunities for teaching and reflection • outcomes: surgical outcomes; teaching/learning: 'reflection-in-action'	• process: in-depth analysis of visual data • participants: non-clinical researcher ('outsider') and surgeon-co-researcher ('insider') • conditions: individual and joint replaying of video data off-site; ample time for close analysis (five days for 1 h of footage) • outcomes: – in-depth understanding and account of material-semiotic dimensions of in situ surgical practice – resources for clinical-surgical training focusing on teaching of critical surgical procedures

(continued)

significantly more detail about in situ practice than conventional ethnographic accounts based on interviews given the gap between what practitioners do and what they can consciously remember and articulate (Greatbatch et al. 2001). The VE study portraying a gall bladder operation revealed the delicate negotiation and embodied learning involving a hands-off consultant surgeon and his trainee attempting to separate the cystic duct from the cystic artery. The analysis revealed the troubled visibility of critical structures, the dynamic complexity of the surgical manoeuvring around these anatomical structures, and the risk-charged trade-offs that permeate these kinds of surgical and pedagogic activities.

For its part, the video-reflexive ethnographic case study revealed infection control behaviours to emanate from largely habituated practices and assumptions rather than practical awareness and considered choices. The VRE enabled the nurses to start asking questions about how they work together now and how they might want to work together in the future. Here, knowledge about in situ practice is first and foremost the preserve

Table 2.2 (continued)

	In situ meaning-making	*Post hoc meaning-making*
VRE case study	• process: clinical teams providing care and conducting infection control practices • participants: multidisciplinary team including medical and nursing clinicians and healthcare researchers • conditions: busy ward, sense of urgency, little to no opportunity for reflection on what is happening • outcomes: infection control conducted with variable levels of risk and unsafety	• process: participative-collaborative visualizing, reviewing and deliberating aspects of practice: 'reflection-on-action' (post hoc) • participants: researchers ('outsiders') and multidisciplinary clinical team members ('insiders') collaborating in visualizing, reviewing and deliberating aspects of practice • conditions: on-site team reflexive sessions focusing on co-selected video clips; six 1-hr reflexive sessions per team (3 teams; 18 sessions total) • outcomes: – team-generated insights into taken-as-given dimensions of practice, and team-initiated proposals for and implementation of practical changes; – video-based infection control improvement and training strengthening clinicians' practical awareness and reflexivity

of the clinicians involved in the study, and is intended to enable them to address local and future challenges, as well as the systemic conditions that give rise to these challenges. This is VRE's potentiation effect: practitioners are enabled to gain a more attentive grip on practice as personal-systemic effect. Finally, a powerful way of conducting research is by harnessing both VE and VRE to engage with complex social and organizational problems. Examples of such mixed endeavours are becoming more common now that the public is accommodating to the ubiquity of visualizations of both everyday phenomena and of specialized organizational practices. We expect social research to make increasing use of these approaches given the rising complexity of contemporary social and institutional life, necessitating more rapid, more local and more multimodal feedback, learning, and intervention.

References

Andersen, H. T., & Stenner, P. (2019). Social immune mechanisms: Luhmann and potentialisation technologies. *Theory, Culture & Society*, 1–25.

Bauman, S. E., Merante, M., Folb, BL., et al. (2019). Is film as a research tool the future of public health? A review of study designs, opportunities, and Challenges. *Qualitative Health Research*, 1–8.

Bezemer, J. (2015). Partnerships in research: Doing linguistic ethnography with and for practitioners. In J. Snell, S. Shaw, & F. Copland (Eds.), *Linguistic ethnography: Interdisciplinary explorations* (pp. 207–224). Palgrave Macmillan.

Bezemer, J. (2020). Meaning, learning and communication in health care: A social semiotic perspective on clinical work and clinical education. In D. Nestel, L. McKenna, G. Reedy, et al. (Eds.), *Clinical education for the health professions: Theory and practice*. Springer.

Bezemer, J., Murtagh, G., & Cope, A. (2019). Inspecting objects: Visibility manoeuvres in laparoscopic surgery. In E. Reber & C. Gerhardt (Eds.), *Embodied activities in face-to-face and mediated settings* (pp. 107–135). Palgrave.

Bezemer, J., Murtagh, G., Cope, A., et al. (2011). "Scissors, please": The practical accomplishment of surgical work in the operating theater. *Symbolic Interaction, 34,* 398–414.

Carroll, K. (2014). Body dirt or liquid gold? How the safety of donor human milk is constructed for use in neonatal intensive care. *Social Studies of Science, 44,* 466–485.

Collier, A., Sorensen, R., & Iedema, R. (2016). Patients' and families' perspectives of patient safety at the end of life: A video-reflexive ethnography study. *International Journal for Quality in Health Care, 28,* 66–73.

Engeström, Y. (2008). *From teams to knots: Activity-theoretical studies of collaboration and learning at work.* Cambridge University Press.

Gilbert, L., O'Sullivan, M., Dempsey, K., et al. (2020). Whatever it takes: A prospective intervention study, using videoreflexive methods (VRM) and enhanced conventional infection prevention and control, to reduce MRSA transmission in two surgical wards. *Journal of Hospital Infection, 25*(3), 140–150.

Goodwin, C. (1995). Co-constructing meaning in conversations with an Aphasic Man. *Research on Language and Social Interaction, 28,* 233–260.

Goodwin, C., & Goodwin, M. (1998). Seeing as situated activity: Formulating planes. In Y. Engeström & D. Middleton (Eds.), *Cognition and communication at work* (pp. 61–95). Cambridge University Press.

Greatbatch, D., Murphy, E., & Dingwall, R. (2001). Evaluating medical information systems: Ethnomethodological and interactionist approaches. *Health Services Management Research, 14,* 181–191.

Hassard, J., Burns, D., Hyde, P., et al. (2018). A visual turn for organizational ethnography: Embodying the subject in video-based research. *Organization Studies, 39,* 1403–1424.

Heath, C., & Hindmarsh, J. (2002). Analysing interaction: Video, ethnography and situated conduct. In T. May (Ed.), *Qualitative research in action* (pp. 99–112). Sage.

Heath, C., Hindmarsh, J., & Luff, P. (2010). *Video in qualitative research: Analysing social interaction in everyday life.* Sage.

Heath, C., Luff, P., Sanchez-Svensson, M., et al. (2018). Exchanging implements: the micro-materialities of multidisciplinary work in the operating theatre. *Sociology of Health & Illness, 40,* 297–313.

Hooker, C., Hor, S., Wyer, M., et al. (2020). Trajectories of hospital infection control: Using non-representational theory to understand and improve infection prevention and control. *Social Science and Medicine, 256,* 1–9.

Iedema, R. (2020). Video-reflexive ethnography as potentiation technology: What about investigative quality? *Qualitative Research in Psychology,* 1–19.

Iedema, R., Ball, C., Daly, B., et al. (2012). Design and trial of a new ambulance-to-emergency department handover protocol: 'IMIST-AMBO'. *BMJ Quality & Safety, 21,* 627–633.

Iedema, R., & Carroll, K. (2015). Research as affect-sphere: Towards spherogenics. *Emotion Review, 7,* 1–7.

Iedema, R., Carroll, K., Hor, S., et al. (2019). *Video-reflexive ethnography in healthcare research and healthcare improvement.* Taylor & Francis.

Iedema, R., Hor, S., Wyer, M., et al. (2015). An innovative approach to strengthening health professionals' infection control and limiting hospital acquired infection: video-reflexive ethnography. *BMJ Innovation.* http://doi.org/10.1136/bmjinnov-2014-000032.

Iedema, R., Jorm, C., Hooker, C., et al. (2018). To follow a rule? On frontline clinicians' understandings and embodiments of hospital-acquired infection prevention and control rules. *Health, 24,* 132–151.

Iedema, R., Long, D., Forsyth, R., et al. (2006). Visibilizing clinical work: Video ethnography in the contemporary hospital. *Health Sociology Review, 15,* 156–168.

Iedema, R., Mesman, J., & Carroll K. (2013). *Visualising health care improvement: Innovation from within*. Radcliffe.

James, D., Hall, A., Lombardo, C., et al. (2015). A video feedback intervention for workforce development: Exploring staff perspective using longitudinal qualitative methodology. *Journal of Applied Research in Intellectual Disabilities, 29*(2), 1–13.

Jewitt, C., Bezemer, J., & O'Halloran, K. (2016). *Introducing multimodality*. Routledge.

Knoblauch, H., Schnettler, B., & Raab, J., et al. (2006). *Video analysis: Methodology and methods*. Peter Lang.

MacDougall, D. (2006). *The corporeal image: Film, ethnography and the senses*. Princeton University Press.

Milne, E.-J., Mitchell, C., & De Lange N. (2012). *Handbook of participatory video*. Rowman & Littlefield.

Moulton, C., Regehr, G., Lingard, L., et al. (2010). Slowing down to stay out of trouble in the operating room: Remaining attentive in automaticity. *Academic Medicine, 85,* 1571–1577.

National Institute for Health and Care Excellence. (2014). Costing statement: Gallstone disease. Implementing the NICE guideline on gallstone disease (CG188). *National Institute for Health and Care Excellence*.

Pink, S. (2007). *Doing visual ethnography: Images, media and representation in research*. Sage.

Redmon, D. (2019). *Video ethnography: Theory, methods, ethics*. Routledge.

Rose, G. (2016). *Visual Methodologies: An introduction to researching with visual materials*. Sage.

Rouch, J. (2003). *Cine-ethnography*. University of Minnesota Press.

Schön, D. (1983). *The reflective practitioner: How professionals think in action*. Basic Books.

Shotter, J. (1993). *Conversational realities: Constructing life through language*. Sage.

Stenner, P. (2018). *Liminality and experience: A transdisciplinary approach to the psychosocial*. Basingstoke, Palgrave Macmillan.

Still, A., & Costall, A. (1991). *Against cognitivism: Alternative foundations for cognitive psychology*. Harvester Wheatsheaf.

Strasberg, S. M., & Brunt, L. M. (2017). The Critical View of Safety: Why it is not the only method of ductal identification within the standard of care in laparoscopic cholecystectomy. *Annals of Surgery, 265,* 464–465.

Thibault, P. (2011). First-order languaging dynamics and second-order language: The distributed language view. *Ecological Psychology, 23,* 210–245.

Vannini, P. (2015). Non-representational ethnography: New ways of animating lifeworlds. *Cultural Geographies, 22,* 317–327.

Wittgenstein, L. (1953). *Philosophical investigations*. Blackwell.

Wyer, M., Iedema, R., Hor, S., et al. (2017). Patient involvement can affect clinicians' perspectives and practices of infection prevention and control: A "post-qualitative" study using video-reflexive ethnography. *International Journal of Qualitative Research Methods, 16,* 1–10.

CHAPTER 3

The Epistemic Use of the Body in Medical Radiology: Insights from Interactional Video-Ethnography

Laurent Filliettaz

Abstract In this chapter, we reflect on the specific instructional practices that emerge when newcomers in medical radiology gain access to such technical skills in the conditions of practice, under the guidance of experienced workers endorsing the role of mentors. The chapter aims at understanding how participants may use the patient's body as resources to navigate complex constraints associated with work procedures and epistemic practices. To do so, we adopt the theoretical perspective of multimodal interaction analysis and we use a collection of audio-video data recorded in a public hospital of the canton Geneva in Switzerland. Video recordings inform naturally occurring work and training practices as they take place during internships in a conventional radiology service.

Keywords Instructional practices · Body · Multimodal interaction · Radiology · Video-based research

L. Filliettaz (✉)
University of Geneva, Geneva, Switzerland
e-mail: Laurent.Filliettaz@unige.ch

S. Grosjean and F. Matte (eds.), *Organizational Video-Ethnography Revisited*, https://doi.org/10.1007/978-3-030-65551-8_3

3.1 Learning Beyond Formal Education

This chapter aims to contribute to the understanding of learning and instructional processes as they take place in the conditions of workplace participatory practices (Koschmann et al. 2007, 2011). Within the literature on vocational education and workplace learning, it is now commonly recognized that workers do not only learn by conducting specific tasks individually; they learn when more experienced workers are able to guide them in their practice, and when adequate resources are made available to them (Billett 2001; Fuller and Unwin 2004; Lave and Wenger 1991; Mikkonen et al. 2017; Tynjälä 2008). From that standpoint, video-ethnography can be seen as a powerful tool to understand how organizations may or not afford learning opportunities through ways of performing situated interactions (Filliettaz 2010, 2011, 2012, 2014). Amongst the resources that are afforded to newcomers, material objects play a significant role in guided professional daily activities. Instructional practices may be directed explicitly to properties of the material environments, and elements of the material world may also mediate the conditions through which newcomers interact with other participants.

These premises seem to be particularly true in the empirical context of medical radiology. When learning to become medical radiologic technologists, students are faced with a wide scope of technical objects, including X-ray devices, scanners or MRI technology. They also have to learn how to position the patient's body so that adequate images are produced for diagnostic or therapeutic purposes. In this chapter, we reflect on the specific instructional practices that emerge when newcomers in medical radiology gain access to such technical skills in the conditions of practice, under the guidance of experienced workers endorsing the role of mentors. We aim at understanding how participants to interactions—including students, mentors and patients—use material resources to accomplish complex and layered actions, oriented simultaneously or alternatively to the production of work and knowledge associated with work. More specifically, the chapter aims at understanding how participants may use the patient's body as resources to navigate complex constraints associated with work procedures and epistemic practices.

To address these questions, we first develop preliminary methodological and theoretical considerations on the relations between situated observable interactions and instructional practices in organizational contexts. We explore different ways to conceptualize the visibility and invisibility of training activities when they occur in the conditions of work. We then present empirical results from a video-ethnographic research conducted in the field of the initial vocational training of medical radiologic technologists. To do so, we use a collection of audio-video data recorded in 2015 in a public hospital of the canton Geneva in Switzerland. Video recordings inform naturally occurring work and training situations as they take place during internships in a conventional radiology service. During internships, students in technical radiology learn to take images of patients' bodies, under the guidance of experienced technologists. Based on fine-grained multimodal transcripts of excerpts of interactions between students, mentors and patients, we describe how materiality pertaining to the patient's body may be used as resources for epistemic practices. To conclude, we return to the question of the epistemic use of the body and materiality in vocational training and outline some practical implications for a better visibility and recognition of vocational training in the field of educational research.

3.2 Interaction Analysis as Research Method for Workplace Practice

The methodological perspective adopted here is that of interaction analysis. Interaction analysis is a multidisciplinary field, borrowing principles from the microsociology of everyday life (Goffman 1961, 1974), ethnomethodology (Garfinkel 1967), conversational analysis (Schegloff 2007) and communication ethnography (Gumperz 1982), whose objective is to describe in detail how individuals coordinate their actions when they are experiencing "social encounters" and collectively engage in goal-directed actions. The interactional perspective recognizes the situated nature of actions accomplished and their underlying psycho-social resources (Lave and Wenger 1991; Suchman 1987). It adopts a constructivist stance and is interested in the collective and temporally ordered dynamics that allow individuals to coordinate their actions with others. Finally, it pays particular attention to the multimodal resources used by participants to engage in interactions (Kress et al. 2001; Mondada 2014). These resources include primarily language and communication, but also pay increased attention to other semiotic modes such as gestures, body postures, visual orientations, symbolic or material objects, etc.

Over the past two decades, the field of interaction analysis has expanded significantly in the direction of work analysis, particularly under the influence of Workplace Studies (Luff et al. 2000) or applied conversation analysis (Antaki 2011). This work has highlighted the centrality of interactions in the accomplishment of professional activities in a wide range of occupations. It also showed how ways of interacting are likely to create specific professional cultures and institutional orders, rooted in specific professional gestures or visions (Goodwin 1994, 2000, 2017).

More recently, video-based interaction analysis has also been applied to the field of initial and continuing vocational education (Filliettaz 2010, 2011, 2014; Koskela and Palukka 2011). A number of empirical investigations have resulted in a fine-grained understanding on how interactional competences are required in specific occupations and how these competences may be developed through guided work experiences, both in formal training contexts (Melander 2017) and ordinary workplaces (Nguyen 2017; Marra et al. 2017). The theoretical principles on which interaction analysis is based have also been transposed into training activities and have been considered as significant contributions to learning and professional development. Moreover, an increasing number of experiences exist, which propose to train professionals in a video-based interactive analysis of their work (Stokoe 2014; Trébert and Durand 2018). From there, interaction analysis can be seen not only as a research method, but also as a tool for practice, and as a medium for designing the "pedagogy of practice" associated with the learning curriculum of workplaces (Billett 2006).

3.3 Instructed Actions in the Workplace

The forms of instructions in the workplace differ in many ways from the teaching and learning practices that can be observed in school contexts. In what follows, we identify different characteristics of instructed actions as they emerge in work organizations and can be conceptualized through different theoretical frames with an ethnographic background.

3.3.1 Instruction as a Framed Experience

One first property of instructed actions is that they must be recognized as such by participants in the contexts in which they emerge. From this standpoint, they rely on processes of "contextualization", produced by participants themselves, and which involve what Goffman (1974) has conceptualized as "framed experiences".

In Frame Analysis, Goffman (1974) shows, for example, that the way people experience the realities they encounter in everyday life is not immediate and transparent but mediated, filtered, by what he calls frames or frameworks. These frames refer to a set of culturally constructed knowledge and skills, called "organizational premises", that allow both natural and social experiences to be interpreted as belonging to a particular type of event, and to answer the question, "what is going on here?". It is by referring to these natural and social frames that individuals produce interpretations of encountered events and that they align their own behaviour to such interpretations. While these frames have a form of existence and stability at social level, the ways they may be applied to specific situations are necessarily distinct and rely on an unpredictable interpretative work. For Goffman, this is what makes the framing of the experience necessarily uncertain and hence "vulnerable". Participants to social interactions can be wrong about what they think is going on in a given situation. They may have to reconsider retrospectively how to interpret a lived experience. Or they may divert or renegotiate the social expectations that govern the current activity. Here again, the use of verbal interactions can be seen as one of the resources by which local contexts can be collectively established and interpreted.

Following Goffman, there are two distinct ways in which a given reality, already meaningful in a primary framework, can be transformed into another activity: keying and fabrication. Fabrication consists of situations in which individuals or institutions produce deliberate efforts to disorient the activity of an individual or group of individuals and which distort their beliefs about the course of events. Self-deception is a possible form of fabrication. The second form of transformation of the experience of reality is what Goffman refers to as keying. Keying refers to a set of conventions by which a given reality, already meaningful by the application of a primary framework, is transformed into another activity that takes the first as a model but that participants consider to be significantly different. This is the case, for example, during drama performances, rehearsals of technical gestures for learning purposes or simulation practices, in which a targeted activity is subject to alterations recognized by all participants.

From a frame analysis perspective, instructed actions in professional contexts can be conceptualized as keyed experiences, namely situations in which a primary frame of work evolves into a transformed experience in which instruction is seen as a meaningful ingredient of what is going on. These transformations and alterations from work to instructed actions must be both accomplished and recognized by the participants. This is precisely what may lead to their uncertain visibility and vulnerability.

3.3.2 *Instruction as an Epistemic Practice*

Instructed actions in workplace contexts involve not only frameworks as meaningful experiences. They also engage knowledge and evolve in the register of what can be identified as epistemic processes. The field of sociology of science has particularly well addressed this aspect of social interactions. Indeed, by adopting a sociocultural perspective on the functioning of science and the production of knowledge, the sociology of science proposes to approach knowledge not as inert objects, but as situated practices carried out by cultural communities (Knorr Cetina 1999). From this perspective, the notion of "epistemic practice" refers to tangible and observable actions by which individuals act on their respective fields of knowledge, whether by sharing, producing, challenging or more generally by establishing such fields as constituent, legitimate and recognizable ingredients within a group. Hence, the scientific community is not the only community in which epistemic practices can be carried out. Working environments are also spaces in which knowledge can be disseminated, according to the rules of use specific to local "epistemic cultures" (Nerland and Jensen 2012; Hopwood and Nerland 2019). From there, particular attention should be paid to the conditions under which work is carried out, in that they can help to understand the processes through which knowledge is produced, circulated and collectively recognized within a community of practice.

Even though there have been little connections between the social phenomenology of Frame analysis and the cultural perspective of the sociology of sciences, compatibilities and continuities can be established between these different epistemologies. Hence, the possibility for participants to share and refer to specific knowledge in interaction depends on how they frame the situation and how they interpret the organizational premises of their encounters.

Recent developments in Conversational Analysis have drawn attention on the epistemic dimensions of verbal interactions (Heritage 2012; Mondada 2013, 2014). Although highly debated (Lynch and Macbeth 2016; Drew 2018), "epistemics" are now recognized as playing a key role in the understanding of the sequential machinery that rules social interactions. For Heritage (2012), the attribution of "epistemic territories" amongst participants in interaction is a necessary ingredient for achieving recognizable actions: "Interactants must at all times be cognizant of what they take to be the real-world distribution of knowledge and of rights to knowledge between them as a condition of correctly understanding how clausal utterances are to be interpreted as social actions" (p. 24). In other words, the very possibility for interactants to create interpretable actions is based on their respective knowledge and the rights and responsibilities they reciprocally attribute to each other with regard to this knowledge. However, these rights and responsibilities are not always symmetrical but often have a stratified character; they require for participants to endorse different positions on an epistemic gradient, which can range from "more knowledgeable" (K+) to "less knowledgeable" (K–). In this perspective, the concept of "epistemic stance" refers to the relative positioning by which interactants recognize themselves more or less aware of certain territories of knowledge. The epistemic status of each participant in relation to the others obviously tends to vary from one context to another, as well as over time. This status can be modified at any time according to the respective interactive contributions of the participants.

From that standpoint, instructed actions observable in professional contexts are only recognizable as such if participants are able to identify objects of knowledge in the environment and to endorse specific and potentially changing epistemic stances with regard to these objects. It is through these adjustments of their reciprocal epistemic positions that participants are able to act on what they consider to be relevant and legitimate knowledge in the context in which interaction takes place.

3.3.3 Instruction as a Multimodal Meaning-Making Process

If verbal interactions mediate the ways participants produce and share knowledge in instructed actions, this is one of many resources used by participants, as non-verbal dimensions of human behaviour as well as elements of the physical environment can play a key role in how participants adapt and interpret their engagement in interaction.

These observations have recently led to extensive research in the field of multimodal semiotics (Kress et al. 2001). The work of Kress et al. develops a multimodal theory of teaching and learning, based on a detailed analysis of situated interactions. The theoretical framework adopted considers that teaching and learning is based on the construction and permanent negotiation a meaning-making process between participants. This conception sees learning neither as a process in which students acquire information directly from teachers, nor as a mere discovery of facts by students, but as "a dynamic process of transformative sign-making which actively involves both teacher and student" (p. 10). In these dynamic processes of meaning-making, participants use a variety of semiotic systems, which Kress et al. refer to as "modes". Meaning constructed in context rarely results from the mobilization of one single mode. On the contrary, it is frequently based on aggregations and combinations of modes, convened simultaneously according to their own potentialities. As mentioned by Kress et al. (2001), "meaning resides in the combined effects of the orchestration of the modes by the producer and the reproducer, in the interaction between what is said, what is shown, the posture adopted, the movements made, and in the position of the speaker and the audience relative to each other in the interaction" (p. 14).

For example, the use of speech makes it possible to refer to abstract content, while pointing at a material object allows it to be tangibly located in space. Hence, the creation of meaning does not consist of switching between successively convened modes, but in a permanent combination and integration of such modes. Another interest for a multimodal perspective on instructional practices resides in the links established between the semiotic choices made by participants and the ways they may exert agency. For Kress et al., "the alternatives that are selected within these networks of meaning can be seen as traces of the sign-maker attempt to choose the most apt and plausible signifier for the expression of meaning in a given context" (p. 12). From that standpoint, teaching and learning can be seen as a material expression of the motivated choices of participants from amongst the meaning-making resources available in a particular situation at a given moment.

From a multimodal semiotics perspective, instructed actions at work may vary not only depending on the degree of visibility conferred on them by the participants through the joint actions they take, but also depending on the semiotic choices made when producing meaning. Consequently, material objects available in the immediate environment can serve as resources for accomplishing instructed action, and not only as means for work production tasks.

3.4 Becoming a Medical Radiologic Technologist

The case study we are conducting here is based on a particular professional context, that of medical radiology. In Switzerland, professionals in charge of producing medical images are certified as Medical Radiologic Technologists (MRT). Medical radiologic technologists produce images of the human body by using different methods (X-rays, scanners, magnetic resonance, etc.) to provide radiologists with the information they need to make a diagnosis. On medical delegation, they also apply therapeutic treatments. Medical radiology has a significant technical component but cannot be reduced to interactions with technological environments. The relationship established with patients at the time of their reception, installation and during the imaging process is a constant concern for medical radiologic technologists, who claim a "care" dimension to the actions they perform in their work.

In French-speaking part of Switzerland, the vocational training of medical radiologic technologists belongs to the tertiary level of the educational system and is placed under the responsibility of so-called Universities of Applied Sciences. To ensure the best possible integration between the theoretical and practical components of training, the existing curriculum aims at an integrative or at least cooperative form of work-related learning: activities proposed within vocational schools establish, through simulation and reflective practice approaches, links with the practical experience accumulated during internships; conversely, internships are supervised by mentors, who have a qualification in the field of vocational training. During their three-year training programme, students complete internships at least twice a year, lasting between 8 and 16 weeks, in different medical contexts (e.g. conventional radiology rooms, scanning or MRI rooms, radiotherapy centres, etc.), whether they are public institutions or private imaging centres.

The situation examined in the following paragraphs was observed during a video-ethnographic fieldwork carried out between 2014 and 2015 in a so-called schoolroom of a conventional radiology centre of a public hospital in French-speaking Switzerland.[1] The "school room" cares

[1] This data was collected as part of the research programme entitled "Becoming a medical radiologic technologist", under the responsibility of Prof. Marc Durand, Germain Poizat and Laurence Seferdjeli, and sponsored by the Swiss National Science Foundation (SNSF).

for real patients and allows images to be taken at all points similar to those taken in the department. However, it has specific features: (a) in that it is equipped with older, less automated equipment, which allows trainees to learn how to make adjustments manually, (b) in that the scheduling planned in this room has a lower rate than that usually in progress in the conventional radiology department. Patients are informed that they are cared for by trained medical radiologic technologists and supervised by qualified personnel. These mediated participatory configurations (Lave and Wenger 1991) allow trainees to manage patients in a way that is strongly facilitated by mentors, and without the temporal contingencies that usually govern the work of medical radiologic technologists.

The observed situation occurs during the first week of the internship of two female students in their first year of training (STU1 and STU2). A patient (PAT) is admitted with a prescription for an ankle X-ray. The patient complains of post-operative pain in this area. A qualified and experienced technologist (MEN) acts as a mentor for the trainee students. She has assigned them the tasks of preparing the image taking, installing the patient, and adjusting the radiological equipment; she supervises the way the students carry out these tasks. For imaging, patients are sometimes lying on a horizontal table above which the "radiographic tube" is placed (Fig. 3.1). The X-rays are sent from the tube, pass through the organ to be X-rayed, and print the image on a "plate", placed under this organ.

The excerpts transcribed below relate to the second radiography performed by one of the students (STU2), under the supervision of her mentor. The task performed here is an X-ray of the ankle profile, including the procedures of positioning the patient's ankle and adjusting radiological equipment before the image is taken. The analysis of these extracts aims to describe how participants engage in interaction at different steps of the adjustment process. In particular, it consists in describing in detail how participants use the patient's ankle at different moment in time during the work procedure and how these uses are likely to contribute to instructed forms of actions. To do so, we successively focus on three types of uses of the patient's body in this interaction: (a) the transformation of framed experiences, (b) the visibility of epistemic territories, (c) and the sharing of a multimodal sensory experience.

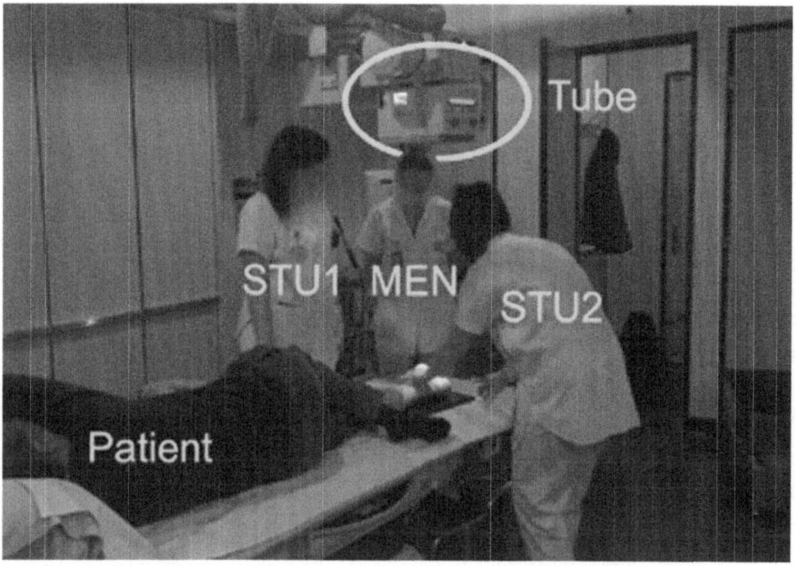

Fig. 3.1 Illustration of the observed situation

3.4.1 Reframing a Work Experience

In this first extract, STU2 has just finished positioning the patient on his side and placing his profile ankle on the plate. She then places the tube over the patient's ankle and makes the necessary adjustments before the image is taken. These operations are scrutinized by both the other student (STU1) and the mentor (MEN).

Excerpt 1: "For me it's correct"[2]

```
STU2:        ((touches the patient's left ankle))
             (adjusts the X-ray tube by observing the foot) [#1]
             there we go\
             ((turns her gaze to MEN))
MEN:         ((turns her gaze to STU1)) (1.7)
all:         ((shared laugh))
MEN > STU1: uh: Alexandra/ ((look at STU1)) (0.4) [#2]
STU1:        for me it's correct yeah yeah
MEN:         so for you it's correct\ (0.2) okay\
             ((sits in front of the patient's foot))
             so/ (0.6) uh + the profile pin so that it's
             in profile what did you look at\
             ((touches the patient's left ankle)) [#3]
STU2:        ((touches the patient's left ankle))
             the condyles\
```

[#1] [#2] [#3]

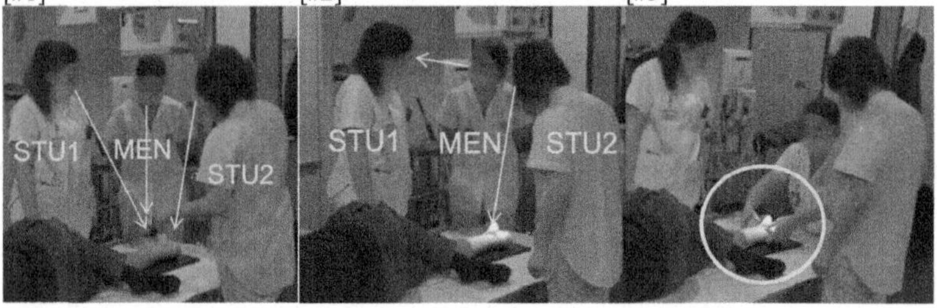

A first type of use of the patient's body in this interaction consists for the participants to act on the local contexts in which their encounter takes place. If framing consists, according to Goffman (1974), to answer the question "What is happening here?", it is noteworthy that this question can receive different answers according to the steps of the extract transcribed above. At first (l. 1–2), the activity frame applied in the context seems to be structured by a set of technical actions, conducted by STU2, under the close guidance of the other two participants (STU1 and MEN)

[2] The transcription conventions are listed in the Appendix.

(see image [#1]). After STU2 has produced a closing marker for its adjustment ("there we go", l. 3), the mentor turns to the other student (STU1) and implicitly ask for her opinion on the accomplished work procedure ("uh: Alexandra/", l. 7). STU1 responds to this request ("for me it's correct yeah yeah" l. 8) and performs what can be interpreted as an assessment action. As this assessment action is ratified and marked as complete by the mentor ("so for you it's correct" l. 9), a new activity frame emerges, in which the mentor takes the floor and gives instructions to the trainees and STU2 in particular ("so, uh, the profile pin so that it's in profile, what did you look at\" l. 11–12).

In this brief excerpt, deep transformations of the micro-contexts can be observed, in which various forms of verbal exchanges between participants take place. These transformations can be identified through a series of "contextualization cues" (Gumperz 1982), produced by participants and used by them as resources to agree on what is going on in the context. These contextualization cues include linguistic markers, which guide participants in the sequential progression of meaningful frames. Some markers act as clues to frame closures ("there we go", l. 3; "okay", l. 9) while others are used to initiate them ("so/", l. 11). But these clues are not limited to linguistic resources. They also include participation frameworks, which act as markers of a permanent reframing of the activity. For example, the transition from the assessment action to a sequence of instruction is marked by a profound transformation in the participatory positions of the three professionals (Goffman 1981): in lines 3–4, the mentor moves away from a ratified bystander position to be placed by STU2 in an addressed recipient position; she is then "invited" by the student to take over the work procedure, which she does by taking on the role of speaker and addressing STU1 ("uh: Alexandra/", l. 7), then STU2 (l. 11–12). Finally, it is important to note that this recontextualization process is also marked by non-verbal cues. Participants use their visual and physical orientations in space to mark transitions and transformations in the ways they frame the situation. They also shift the placement of their bodies in space, which shapes successive activity frames during interaction. For instance, the mentor changes position when initiating instructed actions addressed to STU2: she moves away from a standing position (see [#1] and [#2]) to sit in front of the patient's foot (see [#3]).

In this excerpt, the status of the patient's ankle also does not remain unchanged: if the patient's body is categorized by participants as the target of radiographic activity during tube adjustment procedure (see

[#1]), it gradually becomes a resource and a means of an instruction as the mentor takes a sitting position and begins to touch the ankle from line 11 (see [#3]). At this point in time, palpation of the ankle is used to establish an indexical relationship with the referred material object of an instructional discourse ("so, uh, the profile pin so that it's in profile, what did you look at\" l. 11–12), and no longer to set the position of the ankle for practical image taking purposes. From there, the way participants engage with patient's bodily resources also contributes to bring gradual visibility to an instructional framing of the local situation.

3.4.2 *Configuring Epistemic Territories*

In the following excerpt, STU2 continues to be asked by MEN about the reference points she used when positioning the ankle on the plate.

Excerpt 2: "What did you look at?"

11	MEN	so/ (0.6) uh + the profile pin so that it is
12		in profile what did you look at/
13		((touches the patient's left ankle)) **[#3]**
14	STU2:	((touches the patient's left ankle))
15		the condyles\
16		((touches the patient's left ankle))
17	MEN:	the:/ [the:/
18	STU2:	[condyles the (epicondyles) ((laughs))
19	MEN:	+the:/+ ((leans in the direction of STU2))
20	STU2:	the/ (0.3) e-pi-condyles\ ((touches the patient's left ankle)) **[#4]**
21	MEN:	ankle epicondyles/ (0.3)
22	STU2:	the condyles uh: the uh: the malleoli\ ((laughs))
23	MEN:	((nods in approval of the head))
24		thank you\
25	STU2:	[((laughs))
26	STU1:	[oh\ (0.2) yes\
27	MEN:	it's normal it's the weekend okay/ ((touches the patient's left ankle))

[#3]

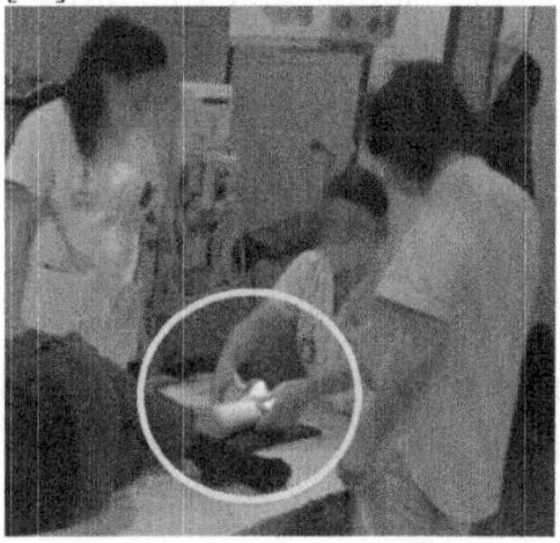

[#4]

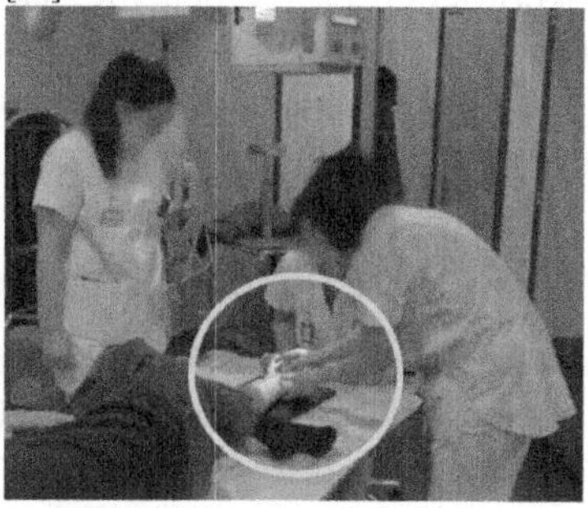

This second excerpt illustrates how the patient's body in interaction may contribute to the accomplishment of an epistemic practice and to the establishment of distinct and asymmetrical territories of knowledge between participants.

Indeed, a conversational activity recognizable as "questioning" is initiated by the mentor at the beginning of this excerpt. These questions take the form of morpho-syntactic structures of an interrogative nature ("what did you look at" l. 12), but they are also marked by prosodic cues and rising intonational contours ("the/the/", l. 17, "the:/", l. 19; "ankle epicondyles/", l. 21). This formation of "questions" is well identified by STU2, who responds by accomplishing "answers" to these questions ("condyles\", l. 15; "condlyes the (epicondyles)", l. 18; "the/e-pi-condyles\", l. 20; "condyles\ uh: the uh: the malleoli\", l. 22). However, since the answers given by STU2 are categorized by the mentor as incorrect, a recurring sequential pattern of Question–Answer is accomplished sequentially, which gradually guides the trainee towards the targeted information: the positioning of a profile pin requires an alignment of the two malleoli.

This sequential organization of turns, typical of an explicit instruction frame, shapes the way in which participants position themselves with regard to their respective territories of knowledge. First, the kind of evaluations produced by the mentor about the trainee's "answers" show that the "questions" accomplished in the situation are not to be considered as "real" questions, but questions for which she knows the answer, questions with known answers as termed by Mehan (1979). But above all, the categorization of these questions as questions with known answers places participants in asymmetric epistemic positions, in which the mentor endorses a role of "knowledgeable participant" (K+) and the trainee that of "less-knowledgeable participant" (K–). The sequential machinery of scaffolding makes it possible to gradually rebalance this asymmetry, but this work highlights the extent to which epistemic issues become a visible and structuring principle at this precise moment of interaction.

3.4.3 *Sharing a Sensory Experience*

The focus on epistemic purposes does not end with the production of a correct answer from the student. It continues with a sensory exploration of the patient's ankle, closely guided by the mentor.

Excerpt 3: "Touch and tell me what you think"

28	MEN:	do you think they are superimposed/ ((pointing of the right index finger on the patient's malleoli)) **[#5]**
29		I have ONE here/ and ONE here\ (1.2)
30	STU2:	mhmm/ ((touches both malleoli)) (1.8)
31	MEN:	look at this\
32	STU2:	[so ((touches both malleoli)) **[#6]**
33	MEN:	[touch them/ and tell me what you think about it\
34	STU2:	no they're not\
35	MEN:	I don't think so either\

[#5]

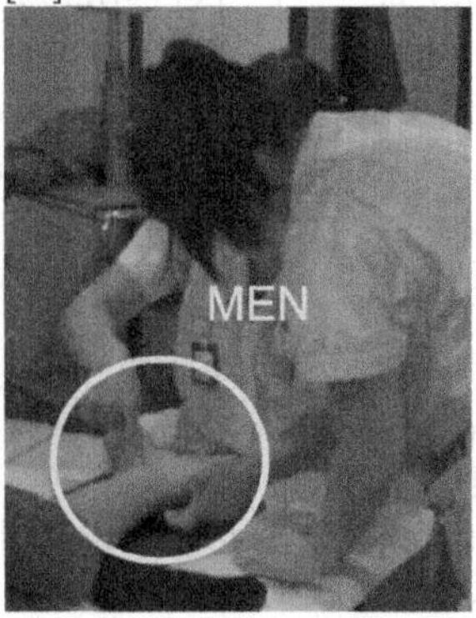

[#6]

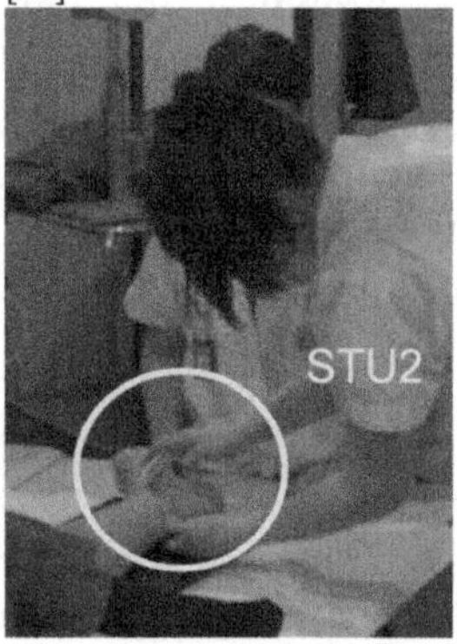

A new epistemic object emerges at the beginning of this third extract, an object brought to the attention of STU2, and which is shaped by the mentor as an experience "to be learned", a learnable in the sense of Zemel and Koschmann (2014). This object consists not only in identifying the malleoli as visual cues required for the positioning of a profile pin, but also in understanding the concept of alignment or "superposition" of the malleoli. Hence, it is not the malleoli as such that serve as reference points for the technician's work but rather their alignment with reference to the vertical axis drawn in the space between the radiological tube and the plate.

Interestingly, the production of knowledge about the concept of "superposition" of the malleoli appears to be strongly situated and is the product of a multimodal experience jointly carried out by the student and her mentor. It is first the mentor who refers to a tangible knowledge of "superposition" in the environment. To do so, she uses different semiotic "modes" or resources of meaning. She first addresses a question to STU2 ("do you think they are superimposed/", l. 28), then an order ("look at this\", l. 31), before completing it with pointing gestures on the malleoli (see image [#5]), commented by an indexical comment referring to the produced gestures ("I have one here/and one here\", l. 29). She also directs her gaze to the patient's foot, creating a visual and attentional space relevant to the students. STU2 responds sequentially to the mentor' invitation by engaging in a multimodal exploration of the patient's ankle. This exploration consists of visual contact with the ankle, as well as a tactile experience of the two malleoli, punctuated by linguistic markers ("mhmm/", l. 30; "so", l. 32). Thus, the student reproduces the tactile experience previously displayed by the mentor (image [#6]). This tactile experience is associated with a knowledge that STU2 explicitly formulates in: "no they're not\" (l. 34). At this stage, she is in a position to infer from the current multimodal experience that the two malleoli are not superimposed.

In sum, this last extract shows how the machinery of multimodal interaction produces the conditions for the emergence of highly complex knowledge in the context, which involves both anatomical properties associated with the patient's body and a specific positioning with regard to technological artefacts involved in radiological imaging. In this local context, the superposition of the malleoli is not only an abstract and generalizable category but is embodied in an indexical relationship to space. It results from a visual and tactile exploration of the patient's body. It is by "touching" the malleoli that participants can learn to "look" if they are superimposed. And it is by learning to "look" at them that they can understand how to position the ankle in the case of a profile radiograph.

3.5 Transforming Work Situations into Learning Opportunities

The case analysed in this chapter shows how medical radiologic technologists are likely to use patients' bodies for epistemic purposes, i.e. to generate, produce and disseminate knowledge about professional practices in the conditions of work. In this context, the patient's body is no longer a mere anatomical object, a vector of theoretical and generalizable knowledge, but an instrument capable of making the rules of action that govern the practice of image taking visible and meaningful. In this perspective, this type of use belongs to what Rabardel (1995) has designated as an "instrumental catachresis", that is, "a gap between the expected and the real in the use of artefacts" (p. 123). Rather than being only the target of a work procedure consisting of making radiological images, the patient's ankle is diverted here from its intended use and becomes the means of another type of activity, that of instructing and sharing knowledge about work.

This highlights the power of participants to influence the conditions in which their interactions take place. By diverting the patient's ankle from its primary instrumental use, the mentor is not only acting on the perimeter of the two students' territories of knowledge. She uses "interactional competences" (Pekarek Doehler et al. 2017) to change the very nature of the action being carried out and the context in which it takes place. In the data analysed above, the practice of instruction is thus particularly visible. This visibility results from the multiplicity of both verbal and non-verbal cues that allow participants to display to each other that what is going on in the encounter does not consist exclusively in the production of a work but also includes the reference to categories of thought about that work.

Video-ethnographic methods in general and interaction analysis in particular are not external to the recognition of the specific nature of instructed actions as they take place in the conditions of work. They can contribute to highlight the fact that educational experiences that take place beyond the perimeter of school practices are not limited to explicit utterances and content-based talk, but also involve a detailed understanding of the psycho-social and semiotic conditions in which these utterances are observable. From our perspective, this is a valuable contribution from the field of multimodal interaction analysis to the exploration of the "boundaries of education" and a promising avenue for research on vocational training.

Appendix: Transcription Conventions

/ \	rising and falling intonation
°xxx°°	decrease in voice volume
+xxx++	increase in voice volume
[	overlapping talk
(.)	micro-pause
(2.1)	pauses in seconds
XXX	inaudible segment
exTRA	accentuated segment
((pointing))	non-verbal behaviour
STU >	direct address to designated recipient
[#1]	location of the image in the transcript

References

Antaki, C. (2011). *Applied conversation analysis: Intervention and change in institutional talk*. Springer.

Billett, S. (2001). Learning through work: Workplace affordances and individual engagement. *Journal of Workplace Learning, 13*(5), 209–214.

Billett, S. (2006). Constituting the workplace curriculum. *Journal of Curriculum Studies, 38*(1), 31–48.

Drew, P. (2018). Epistemics in social interaction. *Discourse Studies, 20*(1), 163–187.

Filliettaz, L. (2010). Guidance as an interactional accomplishment: Practice-based learning within the Swiss VET system. In S. Billett (Ed.), *Learning through practice: Models, traditions, orientations and approaches* (pp. 156–179). Springer.

Filliettaz, L. (2011). Collective guidance at work: A resource for apprentices? *Journal of Vocational Education and Training, 63*(3), 485–504.

Filliettaz, L. (2012). Affording learning environments in workplace contexts: An interactional and multimodal perspective. *International Journal of Lifelong Education, 32*(1), 107–122.

Filliettaz, L. (2014). Learning through interactional participatory configurations: Contributions from video analysis. In A. Rausch, Ch. Harteis, & J. Seifried

(Eds.), *Discourses on professional learning: On the boundary between learning and working* (pp. 317–339). Springer.
Fuller, A., & Unwin, L. (2004). Expansive learning environments: Integrating organizational and personal development. In A. Fuller, A. Munro, & H. Rainbird (Eds.), *Workplace learning in context* (pp. 142–160). Routledge.
Garfinkel, H. (1967). *Studies in ethnomethodology*. Polity Press.
Goffman, E. (1961). *Encounters: Two studies in the sociology of interaction*. The Bobbs-Merill Company.
Goffman, E. (1974). *Frame analysis: An essay on the organization of experience*. Harvard University Press.
Goffman, E. (1981). *Footing: In Forms of talk* (pp. 124–159). University of Pennsylvania Press.
Goodwin, C. (1994). Professional vision. *American Anthropologist, 96*(3), 606–633.
Goodwin, C. (2000). Action and embodiment within situated human interaction. *Journal of Pragmatics, 32,* 1489–1522.
Goodwin, C. (2017). *Co-operative action*. Cambridge University Press.
Gumperz, J. (1982). *Discourse strategies*. Cambridge University Press.
Heritage, J. (2012). Epistemics in action: Action formation and territories of knowledge. *Research on Language and Social Interaction, 45,* 1–29.
Hopwood, N., & Nerland, M. (2019). Epistemic practices in professional-client Partnership Work. *Vocations and Learning, 12*(2), 319–339.
Knorr Cetina, K. (1999). *Epistemic cultures: How the sciences make knowledge*. Harvard University Press.
Koschmann, T., LeBaron, C., Goodwin, C., & Feltovich, P. (2011). "Can you see the cystic artery yet?" A simple matter of trust. *Journal of Pragmatics, 43*(2), 521–541.
Koschmann, T., LeBaron, C., Goodwin, C., Zemel, A., & Dunnington, G. (2007). Formulating the triangle of doom. *Gesture, 7*(1), 97–118.
Koskela, I., & Palukka, H. (2011). Trainer interventions as instructional strategies in air traffic control training. *Journal of Workplace Learning, 23*(5), 293–314.
Kress, G., et al. (2001). *Multimodal teaching and learning*. Continuum Pub: The rhetorics of the science classroom.
Lave, J., & Wenger, E. (1991). *Situated learning: Legitimate peripheral participation*. Cambridge University Press.
Luff, P., Hindmarsh, J., & Heath, C. (2000). *Workplace studies: Recovering work practice and informing system design*. Cambridge university press.
Lynch, M., & Macbeth, D. (2016). The epistemics of Epistemics: An introduction. *Discourse Studies, 18*(5), 493–499.
Marra, M., Holmes, J., & Kidner, K. (2017). Transitions and interactional competence: Negotiating boundaries through talk. In S. Pekarek Doehler

et al. (Eds.), *Interactional competences in Institutional settings: from school to the workplace* (pp. 227–251). Palgrave Macmillan.

Mehan, H. (1979). 'What time is it, Denise?": Asking known information questions in classroom discourse. *Theory into Practice, 18*(4), 285–294.

Melander, H. (2017). Becoming a "Good Nurse": Social norms of conduct and the management of interpersonal relations. In S. Pekarek Doehler et al. (Eds.), *Interactional competences in institutional settings* (pp. 171–196). Palgrave Macmillan.

Mikkonen, S., Pylväs, L., Rintala, H., Nokelainen, P., & Postareff, L. (2017). Guiding workplace learning in vocational education and training: A literature review. *Empirical Research in Vocational Education and Training, 9*(1), 2–22.

Mondada, L. (2013). Displaying, contesting and negotiating epistemic authority in social interaction: Descriptions and questions in guided visits. *Discourse Studies, 15*(5), 597–626.

Mondada, L. (2014). Instructions in the operating room: How the surgeon directs their assistant's hands. *Discourse Studies, 16*(2), 131–161.

Nerland, M., & Jensen, K. (2012). Epistemic practices and object relations in professional work. *Journal of Education and Work, 25*(1), 101–120.

Nguyen, H. T. (2017). Toward a Conversation Analytic framework for fracking interactional competence development from school to work. In S. Pekarek Doehler et al. (Eds.), *Interactional competences in institutional settings* (pp. 197–225). Palgrave Macmillan.

Pekarek Doehler, S., Bangerter, A., De Weck, G., Filliettaz, L., Gonzalez Martinez & Petitjean, C. (Eds.). (2017). *Interactional competences in institutional settings*. Palgrave Macmillan.

Rabardel, P. (1995). *Les hommes et les technologies. Approche cognitive des instruments contemporains*. Presses universitaires de France.

Schegloff, E. (2007). *Sequence organization in interaction: A primer in conversation analysis*. Cambridge University Press.

Stokoe, E. (2014). The Conversation Analytic Role-play Method (CARM): A method for training communication skills as an alternative to simulated role-play. *Research on Language and Social Interaction, 47*(3), 255–265.

Suchman, L. A. (1987). *Plans and situated actions: The problem of human-machine communication*. Cambridge University Press.

Trébert, D., & Durand, I. (2018). L'analyse multimodale des interactions comme ressource pour la formation: le cas du tutorat dans le champ de l'éducation de la petite enfance. In V. Rivière & N. Blanc (Eds.), *Observer l'activité multimodale en situations éducatives: Circulations entre recherche et formation* (pp. 173–198). Editions ENS.

Tynjälä, P. (2008). Perspectives into learning at the workplace. *Educational Research Review, 3*, 130–154.

Zemel, A., & Koschmann, T. (2014). 'Put your fingers right in here': Learnability and instructed experience. *Discourse Studies, 16*(2), 163–183.

CHAPTER 4

The Two-Sides of Video-Ethnography for Studying "Sensing-at-Distance"

Sylvie Grosjean, Frédérik Matte, and Isaac Nahon-Serfaty

Abstract This chapter explores how video-reflexivity is used to study the ways in which sensory information is redistributed by the use of telemedicine technologies. As mentioned by Maslen (2017), making visible the sensory work in context of telemedicine is a methodological challenge. The chapter addresses this challenge with a methodological approach based on the two-sides of video-ethnography. In the empirical study presented, we used a methodological apparatus based on the video recordings of situated clinical activities in telemedicine (video-ethnography called the "bright side") and video self-confrontation with physicians (called the "hidden side"). This methodological approach aims to produce an interpretative framework of clinical practice in telemedicine

S. Grosjean (✉) · F. Matte · I. Nahon-Serfaty
University of Ottawa, Ottawa, ON, Canada
e-mail: sylvie.grosjean@uottawa.ca

F. Matte
e-mail: fmatt3@uottawa.ca

I. Nahon-Serfaty
e-mail: inahonse@uottawa.ca

S. Grosjean and F. Matte (eds.), *Organizational Video-Ethnography Revisited*, https://doi.org/10.1007/978-3-030-65551-8_4

by the doctors themselves to make visible various forms of "sensing-at-distance."

Keywords Senses · Clinical practice · Self-confrontation · Embodied · Multimodality

4.1 Introduction

The year 2020 has seen the hatching of a global pandemic than will certainly impact how we function on a daily basis in the coming years. For instance, physical distancing has brought another level of consciousness to the ways in which our bodies are positioned to one another. It makes emerge the challenge of evaluating the needed space between individuals in regard to the two meters rule, an evaluation that is required to maintain an appropriate distance to prevent the spread of the virus. For instance, two walkers navigating their distances on the same sidewalk will first and foremost be engaged in practices that allow them to be "sensing-at-distance." When someone walks toward another person, there is indeed always the question of timing and who will first divert from its initial (and linear) trajectory and initiate the adjustment.

With these simple but nonetheless necessary physical measures, we are confronted with the obligation of making sense at distance, or, in other words, to assess the situation while moving from afar. Many questions may emerge throughout this distanced sense-making: Does this person look like someone who will cooperate in the adjustment process? Is body language a good indication of the fine-tuning to come (or not)? Does she/he seem aware of the situation or is she frenetically texting on her/his phone without noticing? This process of sensing-at-distance—and through the movement of walking in this case—exemplifies the challenge of evaluating a body from afar by relying on senses and on the plausible cues and signs they offer to acquire an acute reading of the situation. In this short illustration, no devices or tools are used in the process, as it is a matter of direct sensing (i.e., by using mainly sight) meaning that the interaction is not mediated by anything other than the natural retina of the eye. But what happens in a situation where this sensing-at-distance is mediated by a (technological) support that would help conjugates with distance?

Relatively to the story of the two walkers, we argue that telemedicine practices enabling health care and medical consultations to patients through the support of a technological device are also about "managing" distance. Hence, in this chapter we explore what we call video-reflexivity in practice, that is, the process of making visible a (medical) practice through the use of video recording. To do so, we (1) highlight the implication for sensing-at-distance (2) mobilize video recordings to stimulate a reflective process that explicitly solicits the participants' interpretations of their video-recorded interactions.

Recording devices are mediators (i.e., proxies) between patients and health professionals. They can indeed be envisaged as a third party in the equation, no more and no less important than the others (Mondada 2019). In this sense, the technological device—a camera video allowing for health consultations at distance—is considered a fully-fledged constitutive component of this newly formed relationship, an actor in its own right (Latour 1992), as its presence is indispensable for the process to occur. Purposefully, telemedicine begs the central question of how to manage this socio-material relationship's distance relative to its corollary, the "problem" of non-proximity. As such, delivering medicine at distance amplifies a paradox: It underlines the trajectory (Massey 2005) in which it takes place—it's mediated nature through a camera video—but it also creates a closeness as it responds to a forced inaccessibility and ideally, fosters more proximity.

Beyond the complexity behind this management of the distance/proximity dynamic between patients and health professionals, in this chapter, we also wish to investigate the methodological implications of the use of a mediated apparatus in telemedicine. In other words, we wish to explore how it is possible to mobilize video-in-use in order to make emerge a reflexive posture on the mobilization of senses in telemedicine practices. How can video-ethnography help us to better understand "sensory work" in telemedicine?

4.2 Senses and Telemedicine

In their seminal work, Lupton and Maslen (2017) already provided us with fruitful insights into the sensory features of telemedicine by highlighting how the configuration of material, social, senses, and affects play an integrative part in the practice. Regarding what they call sensory work, these authors suggest that:

> Many scholars in sensory studies now contend that the senses must be understood as always and inevitably working together as part of multisensory life-worlds (Paterson 2007; Pink 2015). The perspectives that have been variously referred to as sociomaterialism, new materialism and non-representational theory bring together the interest of sensory studies in sensory engagements with the world, with a focus on how assemblages are configured. Such assemblages are complex entanglements of humans and non-humans, involving objects, space, place, affect and the senses (Thrift 2008; Vannini 2015; Vannini et al. 2012). (p. 1560)

More specifically, Gibson and Vom Lehn (2020) propose that sensory work should put more emphasis on micro-behavior actions and interactions to better grasp what are the implications of senses from a clinical decision-making standpoint. They highlight the centrality of vision (or visuality according to Woodiwiss (2005) as a key component of how individuals "make meaning for and of each other in social contexts" (Gibson and Vom Lehn 2020: 80). From a methodological standpoint, these authors indicate that video represents a mean through which we can analyze how individuals make the social world accountable through vision but also, with resources and affordances such as gesture, gaze, physical objects, and talk (Ball and Smith 2011). Nevertheless, they somehow fail to acknowledge the reflexive posture that ought to be comprised with the use of video recording.

Video recording is indeed convenient to proceed to a double investigation of accountability: firstly, in regard to the many ways individual tele-act through senses (i.e., the medical practice accomplished at distance) and secondly, in the self-reflection process of how health professionals and patients make sense of their own practice through discourse and interactions. In other words, we content that there is an opportunity to explore the methodological apparatus required to empirically show the interactional accomplishment of sensorial work in a reflexive fashion, especially in telemedicine where senses are mediated.

Do to so, we will first develop a reflexive posture that shed light on the research method of self-confrontation. We will then present a case study where of a consultation between health workers and a patient in the context of telemedicine. For the analysis, we will focus our attention on sensing-at-distance and self-confrontation. After what, we will discuss the methodological implications of video-reflexivity in practice by revealing the role of the videos self-confrontation in the process of making visible "sensing-at-distance."

4.3 Video Self-Confrontation as Social Reflexivity

One of the foundations of our research method is video self-confrontation (Mollo and Falzon 2004; Kloetzer et al. 2015). The general principle of the video self-confrontation consists in providing participants—physicians in this case—with the recording of their clinical activity in telemedicine, so that they can comment on it. It is thus a form of "consecutive verbal report assisted by the traces of the activity" (Mollo and Falzon 2004: 532). In this case, the physicians are confronted with the videos of their own interactions with the patients, and by visualizing the recordings they reflect of their practices and communication. They become analysts of their own activity. As a reflexive exercise, the doctors are asked to review and rethink their own behaviors, movements, words, postures, but also, they should question their own expertise, at least their clinical expertise in the context of teleconsultation.

But how we should understand reflexivity in such methodological approach? In order to answer this question, we should contextualize this concept in the larger background of what Giddens (1995a: 4) called "social reflexivity" where "everyone must confront, and deal with, multiple sources of information and knowledge, including fragmented and contested knowledge claims." By participating in this reflexive exercise, doctors are invited to reconsider some of their face-to-face practices and interactions with their patients. They are also asked to consider other forms of knowledge, particularly the role of sensible knowledge (though their eyes and ears) via the mediation of the telemedicine screen.

Reflexivity in this methodological approach means as well a reconsideration of the very notion of specialization. The self-confrontation translates into noting that specialization is not an immutable knowledge, but the "possibility of correcting and revising that knowledge based on the premise of methodical skepticism" (Giddens 1995b: 105). Doctors, both specialists and residents, are called to acquire and expand their knowledge and communication skills to better interact with their patients and obtain the most in the remote virtual consultation.

A third aspect of reflexivity to consider is both its cognitive and non-cognitive dimensions. According to Lash (1995: 163–164), social reflexivity is expressed in the ability to process "mimetic symbols," the images, sounds and narratives as signals having an aesthetical and emotional connotation. The self-confrontation opens the door for doctors to reflect on what we can call "empathetic" moments in their interaction with their patients.

In this regard, reflexivity is not just the moment of "positivist" illumination, but also the moment of "contingency, of ambivalence, of out of control-ness" (Lash 1999: 137), thus of dealing with the unpredictable. Social actors (in our case, the physician interacting with a patient through the technical means of telemedicine) should not only rely on a "logical" reflection to make sense of the virtual consultation, but also on a more analogical rationality informed by the aesthetics, sensations, and relations that oblige them "to find the rules to use to encounter specific situations" (Lash 1999: 3). The method of self-confrontation shows that for those doctors with limited or no previous experience in teleconsultation, the situation was more ambivalent, with unforeseen and "out of control" micro-moments, that require them to adjusting their clinical routine and even questioning the ways they would perform another virtual encounter with a patient in the future.

We can also look at reflexivity from the wider perspective of the organizational setting. The self-confrontation as a reflexive process of the individual participants in the research reveals their actions in the "constellation of enablements and constraints originating both from agents' capabilities and the givenness of the physical and social world that agents understand as the context of their activities" (Banks and Riley 1993: 177). In that regard, the reorganization of the consultation virtual space or the interaction of the nurses as co-agents in the teleconsultation illustrate how this methodological approach enhance our understanding of the organizational elements of such reflexive process.

4.4 The Two-Sides of Video-Ethnography

Telemedicine introduces transformations related to patient/provider communication (Oudshoorn 2008; Maslen 2017). One particular challenge is conducting physical examinations and establishing a diagnosis without direct access to a patient's body. These transformations affect the sensory dimensions of clinical practices because the senses have always involved to assist clinicians in ascertaining the health condition of patients (Grosjean et al. 2020). In this context, we need to understand the ways in which sensory information is redistributed by the use of telemedicine technologies (Lupton and Maslen 2017). But, as mentioned by Maslen (2017), making visible the sensory work in context of telemedicine is also a methodological challenge. We propose to address this challenge with a methodological approach based on the two-sides of video-ethnography.

The research project was conducted with 10 physicians participating in a teleconsultation for a post-operative visit in orthopedics to address a critical issue: how the sensory work of medical decision-making is accomplished during telemedicine visits. In order to bring sensory dimensions of clinical practices into light, an innovative use of video-ethnography was required: the two-sides of video-ethnography. We conceived a method that first captures patient/physician interactions during teleconsultation in real time (Heath et al. 2010; Heath 2011). Then, we allow physicians to "look in" by engaging them in a process of self-reflection (Mollo and Falzon 2004).

Practically, we collected two types of video recordings. The former can be described as "naturally occurring data" in that we recorded orthopedic teleconsultations (the "bright side"). We then used this data (video recordings of the teleconsultations) to provide physicians with a resource to reflect on their clinical practice (the "hidden side"). Immediately after each visit, we invited the physicians to watch the video recording of their teleconsultation and asked them to reflect on how they accomplished sensory work at a distance. During this self-confrontation to their own practices, they explicitly made sense of their clinical judgment processes and sensory experiences that had been implicit up to now.

4.4.1 *The "Bright Side": Video Recordings of Clinical Practices in Telemedicine*

First, we chose to observe and record the clinical practice in real time during a teleconsultation. Through this approach, the researcher proceeded with an in-depth analysis of the activities and the interactions that took place within the natural context. Therefore, analytical methods, borrowed from conversation analysis and ethnomethodology, allow us to focus on samples of interactions recorded on video. Our study goes further than a simple language analysis to include the nonverbal, such as gestures, the handling of material resources, and the way the actors are getting organized within the space. For this reason, we have privileged the video recording of activities because it allowed us to access details of workplace activities. A multimodal analysis of interactions (Mondada 2019; Streeck et al. 2011) was carried out and allowed us to identify various ways of "sensing-at-distance" (Table 4.1).

As we can see in Table 4.1, the methodology allows to take a detailed look of the interactions between the healthcare personnel and the patient in order to reveal different aspects of the sensory engagement in telemedicine consultation. The first interaction focuses on the reorganization of the clinical space to overcome the limits of virtual communication by reframing through technical means the doctor/patient proxemics. The

Table 4.1 Summary of findings based on the multimodal analysis of interactions

Interactional constitution of a "shared place" for creating a sense of co-presence	NUR: Do you want me to zoom in? [...] MD_01: [*NUR zooms in on the incision*] OK, and then let's move it a little over. (1,5 s) Good. (.) OK. (1 s) Very good. (1 s) OK. [*Moves his body to the front of the chair and fixes the screen*] And if you can come out now. (3 s) Thank you very much, keep going, keep going back so we can see each other. [*NUR zooms out.*] NUR: OK! MD_01: Thank you!
Socio-technical arrangements of a "clinical frame" as a way for co-producing "shared sensory cues."	MD_03: XX, what I can see, it looks a little bit red, but two weeks post-surgery, it seems that the incision is well closed, I don't see any sign of liquid, do you see the same thing that I see, it's different? NUR: No, there is no outflow, I don't see liquid either, it's a little bit red, but/ MD_03: OK. And the incision is well closed, there is no opening? [*NUR zoom in on the incision*] NUR: Yes, it is well closed MD_03: OK. Jane, are you able to bend your knees? Bend it about 90 degrees? Or more? [*MD body movements to see the knee and the movements. NUR zoom on the knee*] PT: Yes, maybe a little bit more MD_03: Only two weeks after surgery, that's excellent

(continued)

Table 4.1 (continued)

Embodied engagements for creating an empathetic relationship at distance	MD_01: And, Jane, if you don't mind, I need you to stand up for a second and you can see me [*Gets up, PT gets up too*]. What I'd like you to do is bring your leg nice and straight like that [*Touches his right leg while looking at the screen.*] and turn side [*PT turns sideways to the camera*], yeah, exactly, excellent, thank you. And if we could go down a bit. [*NUR moves the camera down a bit and zooms on PT's leg*] And straighten as much as you can [*Touches his right leg, looks at the screen*] PT: Just a second MD_01: Excellent, good, OK. And then, if you can bend your knee up as much as you can [*Bends his knee up, PT bends her knee*]. Can you go further, good, OK, and then I'll let you sit down thanks. [*Sits down*] And when you bring that up, [*PT sits down*], was it painful? [*NUR moves the camera up, focuses on PT's face.*] PT: U(:)h, I could feel the pulling <OK> that it's tight <OK> But, to be painful, it's not so painful [*Shakes her head from side to side*]

second refers to a cooperative sensory work between nurse and doctor that compensates the impossibility of a direct look or touch by the physician. And the third highlights a coordinated physician/patient action as an empathetic gesture that has both a clinical aim and a humanizing consequence.

4.4.2 *The "Hidden Side": Video Self-Confrontation to Reveal "Sensory Awareness"*

Reflexivity is both a key theoretical and methodological apparatus in our empirical research, a research that focuses on the study of sensory dimensions of practices. Our approach enabled us to highlight the sensory experiences of participants through the use of video-ethnography, thus making visible the sensible and affective dimension of their clinical practices. Especially were the physician's comments on their micro-gestures and embodied interaction during teleconsultation with the patient. As Niemi et al. (2010) stated, reflexivity can be studied as the "process of co-construction of multifaceted and many-layered perspectives together with the participants involved" (p. 138).

The analysis of the video recordings of self-confrontations revealed how the physicians seek to build and maintain a telepresence and to do this, they develop a "sensory awareness" when they are self-confronted to their video recordings. The self-confrontation interviews revealed three dimensions of this "sensory awareness" (Table 4.2). We will describe these dimensions to better grasp the reflection produced by the physicians

Table 4.2 Three dimensions of "sensory awareness"

"Sensing-at-distance together"	– Bridging the information and knowledge gap by engaging the body (Body work) – Embodied engagement for "sensing-at-distance" (memetic acts) MD_02: But I asked her to feel it, is it warm, is it different now than before, and I see her face to look if there is something that doesn't seem normal [...] Because it's thing that we can truly, the way she is talking, the way she is presenting herself, it's the only thing, the only thing that we can see
"Creating a sense of co-presence"	– Visual and auditory watchfulness – Reflecting on one's presence on the screen – Building and maintaining a telepresence MD_05: I want to be sure that they can see my face. Sometimes I say, OK, zoom in a little bit to be able to see each other [...] It's important that they don't feel that they are in telemedicine, and I am in the corner of the room, she cannot almost see me, well I like that they can see my expression.
"Be sensitive to the situation"	– Lack of "Sensory vigilance" – Lack of structure MD_RES03: [...] what I find hard, what I find it's that I did not have a structure. It was question, examination, advice, question, ups, another part of the examination, it is truly...I find myself less organized that when I see patients in the clinic where it is more fluid, I see the patient and frequently I see (his/her) knee at the same time I am talking (to him/her), it's easier [...]

during the interaction as a situated interpretation of sensory experience, micro-gestures and embodied engagements. This reflection requires individuals to make senses of their experience and evaluate it, even if this reflection is also co-produced through the interaction between the participants (physicians and researchers) and the video recording of the teleconsultation. And, this reflective process contributes to make visible a "sensory awareness."

4.4.2.1 "Sensing-at-Distance Together": Video Materializing Embodied and Sensory Engagements

Self-confrontation videos contribute to better understand how the physicians used their own body as an instrument of sensing to reveal the sensory aspects of the clinical consultation in telemedicine. In this way, the video helped to generate sensory impressions through a process of reflection and discussion that occurred after the recordings were made. For example, in the excerpt (Table 4.3), the physician examines a patient's leg (knee) to evaluate its degree of flexibility. He tells the patient to bend her knee, to touch her skin and asks her how she feels while doing these movements. On the "bright side" (teleconsultation), we witness the co-constructed nature of the practice as the physician and the patient collectively enact the situation by mobilizing their bodies and senses (touching and seeing) throughout the consultation (see Table 4.1, MD_01). On the "hidden side" (self-confrontation), we see that the physician reflects on his practice by making sense of the consultation in a way that allows him to put things into perspective: He recounts that he was able to read the situation by relying on his senses, but he also acknowledges that he relied on multiple sources of information to get the picture right such as himself doing the required movement for evaluation in order for the patient to imitate it.

The excerpt (the "hidden side") from the self-confrontation interview reveals how reflexivity contributes to filling the knowledge gaps that the physician faces while doing the teleconsultation. In the following example, we can clearly see how reflexivity transitions from the "logical" to the "analogical" in order to overcome the ambivalence due to the lack of information coming from the physiotherapist (see MD_01.1). The mimetic and sensory quality of the reflexive process becomes evident when the physician explained how he was engaging with the patient asking her to mimic his leg movement (see MD_01.3).

Table 4.3 Bodies as instruments of "sensing-at-distance"

Teleconsultation *The "bright side"*	*Self-confrontation* *The "hidden side"*
Extract MD_01, see the Table 4.1 Video recording of the teleconsultation 	The doctor (MD_01) comments the video on this part of the teleconsultation  MD_01.1: So I wanted to get an idea of her range of motion, but also it's not just how much it moves, but how her muscles can move it. So there's two RE: Okay, this is different from earlier MD_01.2: Yeah. So you could have the nurse go full push [shows on his leg as he straightens it], but here especially, that was a very good test because she was bending it against gravity, so she has to have good muscle strength. And another thing, specifically, I'm watching for, is, uh, best way to explain it, when your elbow comes out to there it stops [shows on his arm as he straightens his elbow], but if it goes to there, you get the feeling, you can see that she was doing this, so I know there's more motion there than just what she was showing me, so it just gives me an idea of, OK, she came to 70-80 degrees, but I can see there's more. So, ideally, if it was, if she had a report from the physiotherapist that said, I can do this much or that much, it's helpful, but without that information, you try to get what you can […] MD_01.3: Uh… For me, it's easier to show as I explain, rather than just, you know, saying, bend your knee as far as you can, some people, like she did with her foot, she bent her leg, not her foot, so then I tried to show her, just to help her understand

4.4.2.2 "Creating a Sense of Co-Presence": Video as Mediation

The process of join observation of the video (physician and researcher) helps the physicians to analyze the interplay between observation of gestures, body movements, and dialogues. During the video self-confrontation, the researcher could focus on specific episodes of interaction by encouraging the physician to comment or explain body movements or gestures. In this case, the video supports individual reflection and contribute to reveal a form of "sensory awareness." For example, in the excerpt (see Table 4.2, MD_05), the doctor explains her way of thinking about her presence on the screen and of creating a close relationship with the patient. To do this, she will be very attentive to her own presence on the screen and she will pay attention to the verbal and nonverbal clues given by the patient.

4.4.2.3 "Be Sensitive to the Situation": Video Re-Enactments

Reflexivity is also a way to consider the ambivalence and the "out of order" of the teleconsultation situation, as illustrated in the words of a doctor during the self-confrontation interview (see Table 4.2, MD_RES03). During the self-confrontation interviews, we also observed how the implicit (or emerging) rules of the new clinical situation (the teleconsultation) are revealed while the physician—in this case MD_RES02—was reflecting about his practice and the role of the nurse accompanying the patient played during the consultation:

> MD_RES02 "[…] If X (the nurse) had not been there, I would have asked the patient, but because X (she) is a nurse, she is, she knows, because she has seen many things like this, she knows how to examine, she can tell me if she thinks that it's infected or not, because if the patient touches (the knee) she (the patient) probably wouldn't know if it's infected or not […]"

In both excerpts, the physicians became self-reflective about their own distant clinical practice and this reflection is enacted through the dialogical relationship involving the participants and their video. By addressing the potential of video-ethnography for revealing sensory dimensions of distant clinical practices, we explored—in this case—video re-enactment (Pink and Leder Macklay 2014). We argue that video recording physician's teleconsultations can provide pathways for an understanding of sensory awareness collaboratively with the participants video re-enactments by inviting physicians to reflect on their clinical practice and experiences. As mentioned by Pink and Leder Macklay, video re-enactments "enable participants to create ways of imagining their self-identities and everyday practices, in which participant reflexivity comes to the fore" (2014: 151). For example, MD_RES03 and MD_RES02 came to reflect on his own experience of teleconsultation and realizes that teleconsultation requires a different structure and organization of actions than face-to-face. Telemedicine is not a replication of existing face-to-face consultation practices, but rather developing new types of interaction with the patients and new ways of sensing and providing care such as collaborating with the nurse and delegating sensory experiences.

4.5 Conclusion

Our methodological apparatus was designed to capture interaction in situated clinical practices (video-ethnography called the "bright side") and expose the actors to their own practices by showing these video recordings (video self-confrontation called the "hidden side"). This methodological arrangement allowed us to make visible the body work and the sensory work (Maslen 2017) done during a teleconsultation. Video self-confrontation as a methodological perspective shows that reflexivity is not only a rational criticism of the doctors' own medical practice, but also a way of developing a critical view of the sensory and interactional dimensions of their teleconsultation. As we have seen in our analysis, the non-cognitive reflexivity becomes clear when the physician verbalized the mimetic and analogic aspects (or the lack of) of their communication with the patient. In that regard, reflexivity prompted doctors to realize the underlying rules of distance clinical consultation, thus the necessary emerging structure and procedures that would allow them to overcome the barriers of a technical mediated communication with the patient.

As we also saw with the previous tables, medical consultations accomplished in the context of telemedicine bright forth many opportunities and challenges. One of the challenges touches both patients and physicians when it comes to not only mobilize sensory practices, but also—and mostly—to make sense of them. In other words, sensory practices in telemedicine have to be carried through a re-enactment process that allows for this reflexive posture. In order to build on the sensory knowledge that is created through a medical consultation, we indeed need to take into account as well as reflect upon the micro-gestures and corporeal engagements that temporarily "channel" and embody senses. It is this very recursive process that gives sense-making "at distance" of embodied senses a crucial added value. By being "forced" to be reflexive due to the impossibility of direct sensing, consultation in the context of telemedicine make emerge the much-needed explicit talk about what patients might feel and what physicians seems to be looking for.

Video-reflexivity in practice contributes to stimulate a form of constitutive reflexivity, the term used by ethnomethodologists to refer to an ordinary routine in which people make sense of everyday activities (Garfinkel 1967; as cited in Woolgar 1988: 21). Indeed, reflexivity in our research has been addressed from a physicians' perspective and this form of participant reflexivity provides the researcher with rich data and contribute to make visible a form of "sensory awareness." This chapter focused on describing the methodological way to reveal reflexivity experienced by participants during interactions involving human (physicians and researchers) and non-humans (video recordings) actors. We call it a process of co-reflexivity to underline the cooperative nature of our methodology, a productive way to highlight how participant reflexivity can contribute to sensory knowledge production.

References

Ball, M., & Smith, G. (2011). Ethnomethodology and the visual: Practices of looking, visualization, and embodied action. In E. Margolis & L. Pauwels, *The SAGE handbook of visual research methods* (pp. 392–413). Sage.

Banks, S. P., & Riley, P. (1993). Structuration theory as an ontology for communication research. In S. A. Deerz (Ed.), *Communication Yearbook* (Vol. 16, pp. 167–207).

Garfinkel, H. (1967). *Studies in ethnomethodology*. Prentice-Hall.

Gibson, W., & Vom Lehn, D. (2020). Seeing as accountable action: The interactional accomplishment of sensorial work. *Current Sociology, 68*(1), 77–96.

Giddens, A. (1995a). *Affluence, poverty and the idea of a Post-Scarcity Society*. United Nations Research Institute.

Giddens, A. (1995b). A vida em una sociedade pós-tradicional. In A. Giddens, U. Beck, & S. Lash, *Modernizaçao Reflexiva: Política, Tradiçao e Estética na Ordem Social Moderna* (pp. 73–133). Editora da UNESP.

Grosjean, S., Cherba, M., Nahon-Serfaty, I., Bonneville, L., & Waldolf, R. (2020). Quand la distance reconfigure la pratique clinique. Une analyse multimodale des interactions en télémédecine. *Communiquer. Revue de Communication Sociale et Publique, 29,* 61–87.

Heath, C. (2011). Embodied action: Video and the analysis of social interaction. In D. D. Silverman (dir.), *Qualitative research* (3rd ed., pp. 250–270). Sage.

Heath, C., Hindmarsh, J., & Luff, P. (2010). *Video in qualitative research.* Sage.

Kloetzer, L., Clot, Y., & Quillerou-Grivoy, E. (2015). Stimulating dialogue at work: The activity clinic approach to learning and development. In L. Filliettaz, & S. Billett (Eds.), *Francophone perspectives of learning through work: Conceptions, traditions and practices* (pp. 49–70). Springer.

Lash, S. (1995). A reflexividade et seus duplos: estrutura, estética, comunidade. In A. Giddens, U. Beck, & S. Lash, *Modernizaçao Reflexiva: Política, Tradiçao e Estética na Ordem Social Moderna* (pp. 135–206). Editora da UNESP.

Lash, S. (1999). *Another modernity: A different rationality.* Blackwell.

Latour, B. (1992). One more turn after the social turn: Easing science studies into the non-modern world. *The Social Dimensions of Science, 292,* 272–294.

Lupton, D., & Maslen, S. (2017). Telemedicine and the senses: A review. *Sociology of Health & Illness, 39*(8), 1557–1571.

Maslen, S. (2017). Layers of sense: The sensory work of diagnostic sense making in digital health. *Digital Health, 3,* 1–9.

Massey, D. (2005). *For space.* Sage.

Mollo, V., & Falzon, P. (2004). Auto-and allo-confrontation as tools for reflective activities. *Applied Ergonomics, 35*(6), 531–540.

Mondada, L. (2019). Contemporary issues in conversation analysis: Embodiment and materiality, multimodality and multisensoriality in social interaction. *Journal of Pragmatics, 145,* 47–62.

Niemi, R., Heikkinen, H. L., & Kannas, L. (2010). Polyphony in the classroom: Reporting narrative action research reflexively. *Educational Action Research, 18*(2), 137–149.

Oudshoorn, N. (2008). Diagnosis at distance: The invisible work of patients and healthcare professionals in cardiac telemonitoring technology. *Sociology of Health & Illness, 30*(2), 272–288.

Paterson, M. (2007). *The senses of touch: Haptics, affects and technologies.* Berg.

Pink, S. (2015). *Doing sensory ethnography.* Sage.

Pink, S., & Leder Mackley, K. (2014). Re-enactment methodologies for everyday life research: Art therapy insights for video ethnography. *Visual Studies, 29,* 146–154.

Streeck, J., Goodwin, C., & LeBaron, L. (2011). *Embodied interaction, language and body in the material world.* Cambridge University Press.

Thrift, N. (2008). *Non-representational theory: Space, politics, affect.* Routledge.

Vannini, P. (2015). *Non-representational methodologies: Re-envisioning research.* Routledge.

Vannini, P., Waskul, D., & Gotschalk, S. (2012). *The senses in self, society and culture: A sociology of the senses*. Routledge.
Woodiwiss, A. (2005). *The visual in social theory*. Bloomsbury Publishing.
Woolgar, S. (1988). Reflexivity is the ethnographer of the text. In S. Woolgar (Ed.), *Knowledge and reflexivity: New frontiers in the sociology of knowledge* (pp. 14–34). Sage.

PART II

Video-Ethnography and Organizing Spaces: Sensing Places and the Multiple Nature of Working Spaces

CHAPTER 5

Practising Diffraction in Video-Based Research

Jeanne Mengis and Davide Nicolini

Abstract This chapter discusses how diffractive methodologies can enrich visual and video-based research methods. In human and social science research, diffractive methodologies aim to expand the understanding of objects of study by creating generative interferences and differences. Our aim in this chapter is to illustrate three ways of practising diffraction in visual and video research. These include (1) reading texts intra-actively; (2) reading the performing of an apparatus through another; (3) creating intra-actions amongst different forms of participation in interventionist research. We suggest that by multiplying our sociotechnical and relational ways of conducting video research and by reading one video-methodological engagement through the other,

J. Mengis (✉)
USI - Università della Svizzera italiana, Lugano, Switzerland
e-mail: jeanne.mengis@usi.ch

D. Nicolini
Warwick Business School, Coventry, UK
e-mail: davide.nicolini@wbs.ac.uk

S. Grosjean and F. Matte (eds.), *Organizational Video-Ethnography Revisited*, https://doi.org/10.1007/978-3-030-65551-8_5

diffractive methodologies help us generate inventive provocations and produce new meanings.

Keywords Diffractive methodologies · Video-based research · Interventionist research · Materiality · Organizational space

5.1 Introduction

Diffraction as a methodology is the practice of "reading texts intra-actively through one another, enacting new patterns of engagement, attending on how exclusions matter" (Barad 2010: 243). The idea was originally introduced by Haraway (1997) in her attempt to promote a view of the world attentive to partial perspectives, heterogeneity, multiplicity and the entangled complexity that characterize living. Haraway was in search of an alternative to the traditional mode of philosophizing (and doing social science) oriented on uncovering originals and essences by drawing on reflection and abstract thinking with the aim of seeing clearly through the distortions that obfuscate the true nature. According to Haraway, this Platonic epistemic stance, which underpins all the "industries of metaphysics..." is bankrupt (Haraway 1997: 268). As an alternative, she proposed using disturbances creatively and intentionally as a way of knowing. She described this approach as diffraction, borrowing from physics, where diffraction is a particular kind of interference when waves overlap and generate new patterns. More specifically, diffraction occurs when waves meet an obstacle or go through an aperture, leaving the waves not to neutralize, but to bend and spread out in many directions. Diffraction thus has become a metaphor for the creation of something new, an alternative, expansive way of knowing in which we produce interferences and diffraction "by design" (Haraway 1997: 273).

The concept of diffraction (Barad 2014) is appealing because it gives the idea that nothing can be truly "reflected back" as it is: every attempt to do so would produce something different. Diffraction thus becomes a method for "reading insights through one another, building new insights, and attentively and carefully reading for differences that matter in their fine details, together with the recognition that there intrinsic to this analysis is an ethics that is not predicated on externality but rather entanglement" (Barad in Dolphijn and Van der Tuin 2012: 50).

The concept of diffraction is particularly promising in the field of visual and video-research. Visual researchers are well aware that once we see, we cannot un-see. Every attempt to reflect back produces something different. There is no final meaning in an image so digging deeper is hopeless. The only way forward is to multiply the views by "moving 'sideways' with the flow of experience" (Latour 2016: 94), playfully create interferences between different types of images, visual methods and sensitivities and build on the effects of their differences. Haraway herself used an image to exemplify diffraction and the first example of the application of the diffractive method is in fact the generative conversation with the paintings of Lynn Randolph, in particular "Diffraction",[1] and his commentaries (Haraway 1997: 273).

However, how diffraction can be used in research practice, in particular in visual and video-based research, is still relatively unclear. This is partly due to the fact that the term has been used often as an evocative metaphor rather than a pragmatic orientation; and partly to the fact that most applications of diffractive methods have been text-based, as for example in feminist theory (Van der Tuin 2011, 2014; Thiele 2014). The lack of practical indication of how to work with diffraction has limited, in turn, the take-up of this concept by the research community of visual and video researchers.

Our aim in this chapter is to fill this gap and illustrate how diffraction can enrich visual and video-based methods. We do so by illustrating and discussing three ways of practising diffraction in visual and video research. As we shall see, diffraction can be used, first, as an interpretive practice by actively juxtaposing different forms of representations (e.g. visual vs. written) and reading different types of "data" and "texts" diffractively. Diffraction can also be used methodologically for data "collection" and "analysis". In this case, the juxtaposition is between research apparatuses (e.g. video recording practices) that are actively played against each other to discover how they make differences and produce contrasting

[1] In the painting, Randolph uses displacement (the figure is located in sci-fi like view of the universe) and interferences (between images; between symbols; between moments in history as the character is depicted as having different ages) to depict the state of ontological multiplicity and messiness characteristic of being a woman. The painting and its sequential re-reading by the painter and the scholar are used to exemplify the generative power of reading texts and images through one another and its capacity to generate new meanings. At the time of writing, the painting was available at http://companionrandolph.blogspot.com (accessed on 26 June 2020).

views. Finally, diffraction can also be used as an intervention method, for example by creating intra-actions amongst practitioners' different forms of participation in video material.

Our modest goal is to show that in all three instances the diffractive practice can bring inventive provocations and produce new meanings; it is "good to think with" (Barad in Dolphijn and Van Der Tuin 2012).

5.2 Practising Diffraction by Reading Texts Intra-Actively

A first practical understanding of diffraction comes from Barad's idea of "reading texts intra-actively through one another" (Barad 2010: 243). A diffractive approach thus involved the "reading and interpreting [of] events of different spacetimes one through the other, for example, 1600 Shakespeare's Hamlet through Marx's 1848 Communist Manifesto through Newton's 1687 Principia attending to how exclusions matter" (Barad 2010: 243). New meanings emerge from the conversation between texts and by paying attention to the fine details and exclusions each of them and their encounters produce. The characteristic feature of this way of practising diffraction is that it takes place post hoc in the domain of reading and interpretation (Kaiser and Thiele 2014). A typical example is the work of Murris and Bozalek (2019). The authors diffractively read three existing books on post-humanism and build on their own feeling and experience to generate a number of theoretical propositions on the experiential dimension of research (for another example, see: Van der Tuin 2011).

In the realm of visual research, adopting an (interpretive) diffractive methodology amounts to taking three steps.

First, it entails becoming aware of the "gaze" that is at work when making sense of still or moving images. According to Copjec (1989) the gaze is a form of culturally constituted visuality that pre-exists the individual subject:

> Between the subject and the world is inserted the entire sum of discourses that make up visuality, that cultural construct, and make visuality different from vision, the notion of unmediated visual experience. Between the retina and the world is inserted a screen of signs, consisting of all the multiple discourses of vision built into the social arena... when I learn to see socially, that is, when I begin to articulate my retinal experience with

> the codes of recognition that come to me from my social milieu(s), I am inserted into systems of visual discourse that saw the world before I did, and will go on seeing after I see no longer. (Bryson 1988: 91–92)

The concept of gaze overlaps significantly (although not completely) with the notion of apparatus. For Barad, an apparatus is the set of "material-discursive practices (...) with which we engage with the world" and which are "productive of (and part of) the phenomena" we study (Barad 2003: 819). For example, Aarsand and Forsberg (2010) conducted a video-ethnographic study on the everyday lives of middle class, dual-earner families. They show that "corporeal privacy" is not a given phenomenon open to observation. Rather, the boundary between public and private is produced through their "scientific apparatus", that is the everyday video methodological practices which included the material frames, the objects present, the discourses on privacy, and the interactive negotiations when to turn on and off the camera while in the homes of their research subjects.

This suggests that simply becoming aware of the social and historical situatedness of our gaze and practices of seeing is not sufficient. As researchers, in fact, we cannot operate by subtraction, that is, we cannot resolve the issue by trying to factor out the apparatus itself. What is required is a second step in which we mobilize an alternative gaze. In so doing, we immediately generate a number of interferences between gazes. The immediate effect is that of bringing to attention the existence of the gaze itself. For example, Hultman and Taguchi (2010) propose a diffractive reading of images of children in playgrounds that juxtaposes the traditional gaze (child playing in the park) with what they call a relational materialist gaze ("The girl is in a state of becoming with the sand, and the sand is in a state of becoming with the girl", p. 530). The diffractive reading allows for foregrounding the anthropocentric nature of most current practices of taking and consuming pictures of children. It allows for advancing an understanding of children and park to be differently entangled phenomena, which in turn encourages us to view education not so much as filling a lack but rather offering children supplements and extensions (Lee 2001).

The mobilization of the second gaze thus becomes generative of new and unexpected meaning. This can be achieved, however, only if we utilize a positive rather than negative view of difference—a view in which difference is not understood as a form of absence or lack but rather a generative force (Deleuze 1990). In clearer terms, the second gaze is not mobilized to identify the "shortcoming" of the first one, but rather to generate new possibilities. This in turn requires a third and closely related step is which the two gazes (and the visual representation) are put in conversation and played one through the other. Diffraction creates thereby creative provocations, which makes it is generative, not subtractive. The result is a richer form of understanding that is multiple, irreversible and potentially endless. It is multiple in that the goal is not that of constructing a stable and unified view of the phenomenon, but rather that of generating a crowd of representations that can foster understanding. It is irreversible in that each reading builds on the previous one—so that the differences themselves continue to change. It is open-ended and potentially endless in that the game of interpretation can continue until practical or political reasons stop the conversation such that one of the versions is affirmed as the final and truthful one.

Yet, this first way of practising diffraction also has its limitations. Reading texts, images or other forms of visual representation through one another post hoc still takes place in the realm of discourse. While this post hoc diffractive movement is useful to generate new and unexpected meanings, is it also scarcely attentive to the constitutive dimension that material apparatuses have in the constitution of the representation itself. For example, in the cases above, Hultman and Taguchi (2010) utilize pictures taken by a "professional photographer" (p. 527). This goes contrary to Barad's view, which suggests that the gaze is not in the eye of the interpreter but rather lies at the encounter between the eye of the photographer, the camera, photographic practice, and the practices of interpretation of the viewers. In clearer terms, post hoc diffraction can be accused of trying to close the stable after the horses have bolted. As such, it can be subject to the same criticisms levelled at traditional reflection and perspectivism: that in the world of (scholarly) discourse, it is rather easy to move from one position to another, from one sensitivity to another, from one gaze to another.

We recently found ourselves being caught up in such a mostly discursive, post-doc way of practising diffraction until we realized that we had to go back into the field. We had resubmitted a paper in which we utilized photographs to discuss the inclusion of non-corporate spaces (e.g. public spaces) into organizational spaces and analysed how affective atmospheres emerged in-between different spaces (De Molli et al. 2019). The reviewers were not pleased with the visual material we had provided in the paper. One "found the use of illustrative images to be dull" and not expressive of the affective atmosphere we wanted to show. Thus, we went back to our dataset of over 2000 pictures, taken during our ethnographic observations, with the intention to identify some better-suited pictures. We tried first to simply change pictures and select more "expressive" ones. Yet, as we viewed these images now through the verdict of the reviewer—and no longer, as before, primarily through our embodied experience as observers—we had to agree: the pictures were somehow flat, devoid of the affective, atmospheric charge we felt the space had when walking through it in person.

We could not solve the issue by reading our already collected data one through the other, but had to return to the field. We paid attention to how we took pictures, viewed them through our earlier takes, through the comments by the reviewers, and through our own embodied experience. We started to experiment with short videos, walking with video from one space and atmosphere to another. We did the same by taking extensive ethnographic notes of these passages. With time—and through this diffractive practice of intra-actively reading one rendering through the other—pictures, ethnographic notes, the video material, and our own embodied experience changed, and new patterns and meanings emerged.

By taking into account materiality more seriously (through our bodies, through our technical choices of how to take pictures), we needed to practice diffraction differently (as we will exemplify below), not just relying on reading texts intra-actively, one through the other. Barad (2007) underlines the importance of such material engagement when practising diffraction:

> ...the point is not merely that knowledge practices have material consequences but that practices of knowing are specific material engagements that participate in (re)configuring the world. Which practices we enact matter-in both senses of the word. Making knowledge is not simply about making facts but about making worlds, or rather, it is about making specific worldly configurations-not in the sense of making them up ex nihilo, or out of language, beliefs, or ideas, but in the sense of materially engaging as part of the world in giving it specific material form. (Barad 2007: 90)

Barad utilizes the image of (agential) cut to indicate that setting up or adopting a specific apparatus is a form of "ethico-onto-epistemological commitment" that operates specific cuts in what phenomenologically presents itself. Diffraction thus requires us to understand how different apparatuses and the cuts that they produce "matter in the reiterative intra-activity of worlding, that is, of the entanglement of spacetimematterings" (Dolphijn and Van Der Tuin 2012: 46). This leads us to a second and slightly different practical understanding of diffraction in which diffraction does not take place post hoc but operates earlier when we choose, set up and enact our practices of visual capturing (filming, taking pictures, painting). Diffraction thus starts with juxtaposing research apparatuses (e.g. video recording practices) that are actively co-located to provide contrasting views or played against each other to discover how they make a difference.

5.3 Practising Diffraction by Reading the Performing of an Apparatus Through Another

Diffraction can also be understood as "a process of paying attention to the ways in which practices [of data collection and analysis] produce (…) 'cuts' that can interrupt and splinter the object of study" (Uprichard and Dawney 2019: 19). When Barad reminds us that a phenomena does not exist ex-ante, but is produced in the intra-action with the apparatus (Barad 2003: 819), the implication is that different methodological practices, including not only interpretative, but also material practices, will produce the phenomena differently. To explain this, she refers to the "two-slit diffraction experiment" in quantum physics, which the Nobel Prize physicist Bohr used to determine whether light is a particle or a wave (Kaiser and Thiele 2014: 165). Importantly, depending on the apparatus through which light is measured, its nature changes with light behaving both as wave and as a particle. The phenomena under examination are produced differently in its intra-action with the distinct apparatus that "measures" it. In this way, "[d]iffraction patterns record the history of interaction, interference, reinforcement, difference. Diffraction is about heterogeneous history, not about originals" (Haraway 1997: 273).

Indeed, when deploying mixed methods in data collection, we can produce multiple "cuts" of the object of study, which might not be integrated into a coherent whole as the method is usually practised, but rather propose an opportunity for a diffractive reading (Uprichard and Dawney 2019: 20). Paying attention to the differences that are produced through the different methods with which we approach our object of study, we can become attentive to its different qualities and ways of being (in the light example above, a wave and a particle). Second, as we will show below, it can also be useful to learn about the performativity of our methodological choices. And finally, by diffractively reading one production of the object of study through another, we can become aware of the "interferences" and "reinforcement[s]" of our methodological practices (Haraway 1997: 273).

To exemplify such a diffractive methodology and their benefits in video-based research, we will refer to an "experiment" we conducted to better understand the specific performances of the apparently technical choices of camera angle and movement on our object of study (for details of the study, see Mengis et al. 2018). The "experiment" consisted in conducting three observational studies in healthcare settings, focusing on interprofessional coordination practices in the emergency department of a regional hospital in Switzerland, interaction practices between patients and clinicians in a dental outpatient clinic in Northern Italy and later the patient journey in a A&E department in the UK.[2] All involved video-based observations of interactions. When reviewing the video recordings of our first two settings, we realized that space was an important mediator of the interactional practice; space was constantly rearranged through the displacement of machinery, utensils, furniture, the drawing of curtains, and the collective movement of people in space, thus shaping the coordination and interaction of people. As we tried to inquire into this issue also in the second context, we found—to our surprise—that the video recordings did not foreground space equally.

As recordings of the two contexts were similar for the movements of people and objects, but different for the deployment of camera angles—one working with a wide-angle shot, the other with a medium shot—we started to inquire whether camera angles matter for how space is performed as a phenomena. From previous studies on organizational space (for recent overviews, see Beyes and Holt 2020; Stephenson et al. 2020), we knew that space is not just one "thing" and limited to its physical layout, but rather is multiple and processual. Space continues to be produced (Lefebvre 1974/1991) in interaction with people's spatial practices (what Lefebvre calls "perceived space", e.g. employees' habitual missions to the coffee machine) and their ways of making sense of space (what Lefebvre calls "lived space", namely the way people give

[2] For reasons of space only the first two studies made it into the final paper.

meaning to space in relation to, for example, foregone spaces of the past or to collective imaginations of an "office" space). Our initial video-recordings seemed to suggest that the technical choices of how video data are recorded or viewed may be of methodological relevance to how a phenomena can be studied (Laurier 2013; Luff and Heath 2012; Mondada 2009), or in our case to how space would manifest (as a practised space, as a lived space). The question was how exactly this happened and how the technical choices of our recordings mattered for how space would be produced "differently".

In a second part of the study, we video-recorded the clinical practice with different camera angles and added a third site in the UK. With the steady camera, we worked both with wide-angle and mid-angle shots and further experimented with a roving camera, either following the mobile action of practitioners by walking next to them or attaching a head-camera on their forehead (Laurier 2013; MacBeth 1999; Pink 2007). We thus experimented with four different video recording apparatuses: the Panoramic View (a steady camera using a wide-angle shot), the American-Objective View (a steady camera using a mid-angle shot), the Roving Point-of-View (a roving camera tracing the clinical practice by following practitioners cheek-to-cheek), and the Infra-Subjective View (a head-mounted camera on a practitioner tracing the clinical practice for a subjective angle) (Mengis et al. 2018).

When analysing these recordings, we started to engage in a diffractive practice focusing on the differences the four apparatuses produced in how organizational space revealed itself. We found that each video recording apparatus privileges a different spatial understanding (see Fig. 5.1). For example, the Panoramic View pointed to space as physical extension (e.g. objective positions of objects/people in space) and privileged a structural explanation of space as the materialization of power (e.g. how spaces are joined/divided, control of entry/location). Instead, the Roving-Point-of-View foregrounded a collectively practised space where space is assembled through rhythmic spacing, through directionalities and orientations of objects and bodies, and through activities within space.

It is important to note that these different performances were not only produced by the specific video-recording practices, but also by our diffractive reading of one recording and its apparatus through the other. The panoptic, refrained gaze of the Panoramic view with its privileging a focus on structure, control, or resistance emerged by viewing it through the Roving Point-of-View and its performances. At the same time, the Roving

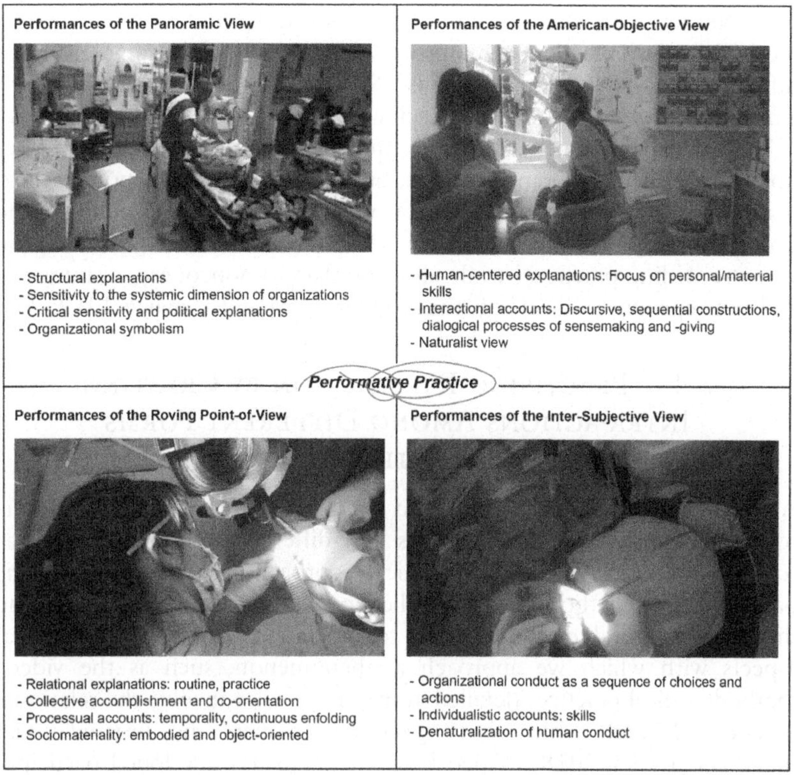

Fig. 5.1 Diffractively viewing different video recording apparatuses one through the other (on the basis of Mengis et al. 2018)

Point-of-View's focus on embodied effort, processual enfolding and materially oriented practice emerged by viewing these recordings through the ones of the American-Objective View and the Infra-Subjective View. By viewing the recordings of the different apparatuses one through the other, we could "attend (...) on how exclusions matter" (Barad 2010: 243), that is which qualities of space emerged and which ones faded into the background. In this way, the different video-recording apparatuses had not fixed performances (cp. notion of "affordances", Gibson 1977; Majchrzak and Markus 2012), but as the apparatuses became entangled with our diffractive practice, specific differences (of space) were produced.

A diffractive practice is thus importantly different from the general methodological practice to compare and contrast, for example, across different data collection methods. Such a methodological approach aims to "integrate" data and to achieve "valid" and "reliable" findings (Uprichard and Dawney 2019: 28). Instead, the diffractive method does not focus on the coherence of data, but rather allows a phenomenon to manifest in multiple ways. It is in this way that diffraction "splinters" the object of study, inviting us to read "data across methods [and multiple video recording practices] while allowing data to noncohere, disintegrate and not reproduce objects of study" (Uprichard and Dawney 2019: 29).

5.4 Practising Diffraction by Creating Intra-actions Among Different Forms of Participation in Interventionist Research

A third way of understanding and practising a diffractive method is to create interferences, interactions and differences through participatory research, that is, methodological approaches that involve participants in the field both in data collection and in analysis. Indeed, the diffractive method does not need to be limited to the sociotechnical aspects with which we approach a phenomenon, such as the video-methodological practices detailed above. It can also involve the relational practices through which we engage practitioners and organizational members (Bayley 2018). Video-based research has developed participatory approaches by involving organizational members in the analysis of the video material in which they were recorded in the first place (Milne et al. 2012; Whiting et al. 2018). For example, Jarrett and Liu (2016) present a "zooming with" method where excerpts of their video material are proposed to the individuals involved in the recording. They used the video clips for a "projective interview", which allowed them to understand the participants' interpretations of the recorded scenes and grasp "their recollections, motives, and feelings" (pp. 374–375). Their interest in drawing on the interpretation of participants was to be able to "integrate" (Uprichard and Dawney 2019) the various interpretations of participants as well as their own.

Participatory approaches in video research can, however, also be used with a diffractive attitude. An interesting example is proposed by

Ivinson and Renold (2016). Working in a former coal-mining community in Wales, the authors used a diffractive analysis to explore the notions of gender and corporeality of teenage girls. After a more traditional, interview-based study on "Young People and Place", the scholars returned to the schools where they had conducted the interviews and recruited two girls to participate in a film project. Together, they developed the idea of what they were going to film (the girls would run), and where (a park where they used to jog, but whose woods were considered dangerous because of stories of rape and abduction). The short "Still Running" was filmed during the course of one day; the girls were video recorded by the two female researchers and a professional filmmaker in a park while running, a practice they had enjoyed in pre-adolescence, but no longer (p. 172). While filming, the girls initially felt very conscious of the "objectifying male gaze" (p. 181), running slowly and protecting their chest with their arms to prevent their breasts from moving. Realizing their discomfort, the scholars decided to participate themselves in the running, "unashamedly" and secure of themselves (p. 175). This, together with the "anonymous gaze" of the camera and the camera women—enacted in the ritual of repeatedly setting up the tripod and installing the camera for the next shot (and diffracted by readings of Deleuze 1985/1989)—let the "ubiquitous sense 'of always being watched' by an imaginary predatory male be neutralized" (p. 178). By running and re-running the same path, the girls gradually inhabited their bodies "more fully" and sprinting became "bolder and faster" (p. 178). Through the collective, female entanglements with the camera and the girls' repeated running, a "girl-body-camera-landscape assemblage" was co-produced (p. 182). It allowed for a transition from stuckness to fluidity, a fluidity that temporarily interrupted the dominant production of the female within the post-industrial places of coal-mining where gendered legacies of masculine corporeal strength and movement (p. 170) blocked the girls in becoming energetic and being in their bodies.

The example shows how the embodied, space-bound, technically mediated, but also relational intervention by the scholars provoked multiple diffractions with historical legacies of masculinity and femininity, ongoing gender-based bullying in schools, present internalized gazes, and practices from the personal past (pre-adolescent jogging). Diffraction here is not practised by the researchers and their methodological choices and technical equipment alone, but also involves the participants and their intra-active responding, their choice of activity and location, their bodily discomfort, their growing confidence. The object of study thereby continued to emerge in the diffractive practice as notions of gender and corporeality were not fixed, but evolved both in the embodied, video-based practice of the girls and of the scholars.

A second example, this time rooted in an organizational work setting, is offered by the work of Rick Iedema and his colleagues (Iedema et al. 2006, 2018). The group has been experimenting with participatory video-based research in healthcare settings for a decade. Over the years, they have developed a well-thought-out process for using video in a collaborative fashion, both for academic purposes and for the improvement of clinical practice.

The scholars spend initially sometime in the hospital to observe a particular practice—for example, the handover between two clinical teams (for details, see Iedema et al. 2006, 2018). After obtaining permission, they then film aspects of the handover practice during three weeks. The researchers edit instances they found relevant and then show them to the various groups involved in the handover, such as the intensive care unit team and the surgery team. These separate viewings allow for different aspects, priorities, and meanings to emerge. On the basis of these multiple accounts, the scholars then select some relevant scenes to be shown to the whole group of people involved in the handover. The video excerpts are now being discussed within this inter-professional and interdisciplinary context, such that the different emerging interpretations and concerns diffract one through the other as well as with the ones of the researchers. On this basis, the practitioners develop together concrete measures to improve their practice and after some weeks that the new practice had been implemented, they do another round of video recordings and diffract these with the former practice (Iedema et al. 2006).

Such an approach resounds the interventionist methods developed in the context of activity theory, which can provide further theoretical depth. For example, Yves Clot's "clinic of activity" (Clot 2009) proposes to video record sequences of work activity (e.g. work on assembly lines, delivering homilies), to then use to confront protagonists of the activity in individual settings (simple self-confrontation) as well as to subsequently call for collective discussions between pairs of workers and amongst the whole team involved (cross self-confrontation). All these dialogic activities are themselves video-recorded. The aim of the approach therefore is not to get to the essence of the activity. Rather, through the dialogic practice around the video artefact, "professional dispute" and "controversy" (Kostulski and Kloetzer 2014) are orchestrated with the aim of unleashing the development of the activity. In this way, the approach should enable workers to relate in another way to their work "by seeing things differently – through the eyes of the others" (Kloetzer et al. 2015: 62). Consequently, the approach foresees that out of this dialogic practice a "multi-voiced" film is produced that can bring about further conversations at other levels of the organization (Kloetzer et al. 2015: 52).

In such participatory, interventionist approaches (see also: Mesman 2011; Mesman et al. 2019), we can find many of the diffractive qualities discussed so far. The methods are geared towards multiplying the object under analysis (Uprichard and Dawney 2019), actively giving different practitioners the possibility to develop their own understanding so that their different readings can interact, interfere, reinforce, or differ without necessarily having to integrate into a coherent whole. The approaches also acknowledge the processual, evolving nature of phenomena as the interventions in practice and their diffractive readings are recurring over time (e.g. there is no right handover, but the phenomenon continuously evolves).

Taken together, the two examples illustrate a third way of practising diffraction. Unlike the former two, participative diffraction entails a working with and through the participants in the field, their practices, their tools, bodies, and discourses, performing cuts to the object of study in intra-action.

5.5 Concluding Remarks

Bruno Latour (2002) once commented that we should avoid "freeze-framing" and "extracting an image out of the flow, and becoming fascinated by it, as if it were sufficient, as if all movement had stopped" (p. 22). He adds that "the only way to access truth, objectivity, and sanctity is to move fast from one image to another, not to dream the impossible dream of jumping to a non-existing original" (Latour 2002: 22). In this chapter, we have illustrated three ways in which this can be achieved by mobilizing the conceptual and practical toolbox of diffraction. As we have shown, diffraction is both a powerful heuristic and a sophisticated methodological resource.

As a heuristic, when used proactively and generatively, diffraction helps to illuminate "the complexity of the always/already entangled processes of dis/continuous becomings that make up what we are used to calling world" (Thiele 2014: 207). It does so by placing different transdisciplinary practices in conversation with one another "whilst paying attention to fine details and the exclusions this action produces" and "by investigating how 'objects' and 'subjects' and other differences matter, and for whom" (Barad 2007: 90–94).

As a methodological resource diffraction alerts against a reductive understanding of reflexivity. Increasingly, reflexivity is conceived merely as the effort to recognize the "situatedness of knowledge" and the performative interference of the methods and apparatuses we use. The ensuing injunction is that when we choose an apparatus or method we need to remain reflexive of what is left out, what the apparatus does not make us see. This understanding of reflexivity as lack and incompleteness may suggest that we can solve the issue by subtraction: if we factor out the gaze and apparatus from the representation (or, in the case of research, disentangle the methodologies used to collect and analyse data and the subjectivity of the researcher), we can get to the bottom of things—the essence of meaning. Diffraction warns that such an attempt is destined to fail. "Data" are always the result of an intra-action between phenomena and apparatuses; "reflecting back" on the source of data does not get us close to the real thing as we have seen in our examples above: every attempt to do so produces something different and new. Although as noted by Lumsden (2019), the contraposition between reflexivity and diffraction upheld by some authors is rather contrived (good reflexivity has always been non-subtractive), diffraction invites to embrace rather than fear our incompleteness. Diffraction both as a metaphor and as a practice invites us to embrace the idea that good science (and social science) is about adding meaning and complexifying our appreciation of the world rather than succumbing to traditional eliminativist and reductive approaches that invite and often pressure us into "abstracting or deconstructing" rather than expanding and creating (Stengers 2008: 3).

References

Aarsand, P., & Forsberg, L. (2010). Producing children's corporeal privacy: Ethnographic video recording as material-discursive practice. *Qualitative Research, 10*(2), 249–268.

Barad, K. (2003). Posthumanist performativity: Toward an understanding of how matter comes to matter. *Signs: Journal of women in culture and society*, *28*(3), 801–831.

Barad, K. (2007). *Meeting the universe halfway: Quantum physics and the entanglement of matter and meaning*. Duke University Press.

Barad, K. (2010). Quantum entanglements and hauntological relations of inheritance: Dis/continuities, spacetime enfoldings, and justice-to-come. *Derrida Today*, *3*(2), 240–268.

Barad, K. (2014). Diffracting diffraction: Cutting together-apart. *Parallax*, *20*(3), 168–187.

Bayley, A. (2018). *Posthuman pedagogies in practice: Arts based approaches for developing participatory futures*. Palgrave.

Beyes, T., & Holt, R. (2020). The topographical imagination: Space and organizational theory. *Organization Theory*. https://doi.org/10.1177/2631787720913880.

Bryson, N. (1988). The gaze in the expanded field. In H. Foster (Ed.), *Vision and visuality* (pp. 87–108). Bay Press.

Clot, Y. (2009). Clinic of activity: The dialogue as instrument. In A. Sannino, H. Daniels, & K. Gutiérrez (Eds.), *Learning and expanding with Activity Theory* (pp. 286–302). Cambridge University Press.

Copjec, J. (1989). The orthopsychic subject: Film theory and the reception of Lacan. *October*, *49*, 53–72.

De Molli, F., Mengis, J., & van Marrewijk, A. (2019). The aestheticization of hybrid space: The atmosphere of the Locarno Film Festival. *Organization Studies*. https://doi.org/0170840619867348.

Deleuze, G. (1985/1989). *Cinema 2: The Time Image* (H. Tomlinson & R. Galeta, Trans.). University of Minnesota Press.

Deleuze, G. (1990). *The logic of sense* (M. Lester, Trans.). Columbia University Press.

Dolphijn, R., & Van Der Tuin, I. (2012). Matter feels, converses, suffers, desires, yearns and remembers: Interview with Karen Barad. *New Materialism: Interviews and Cartographies*, 48–70. http://doi.org/10.3998/ohp.11515701.0001.001.

Gibson, J. J. (1977). The concept of affordances. In R. Shaw & J. Bransford (Eds.), *Perceiving, acting, and knowing* (pp. 67–82). Lawrence Erlbaum.

Haraway, D. (1997). Modest_Witness@Second_Millennium. FemaleMan© Meets_OncoMouse™. In *Feminism and Technoscience*. Routledge.

Hultman, K., & Taguchi, H. L. (2010). Challenging anthropocentric analysis of visual data: A relational materialist methodological approach to educational research. *International Journal of Qualitative Studies in Education*, *23*(5), 525–542.

Iedema, R., Carroll, K., Collier, A., Hor, S. Y., Mesman, J., & Wyer, M. (2018). *Video-Reflexive Ethnography in Health Research and Healthcare Improvement: Theory and Application*. CRC Press.

Iedema, R., Long, D., Forsyth, R., & Lee, B. B. (2006). Visibilising clinical work: Video ethnography in the contemporary hospital. *Health Sociology Review, 15*(2), 156–168.

Ivinson, G., & Renold, E. (2016). Girls, camera, (intra) action: Mapping posthuman possibilities in a diffractive analysis of camera-girl assemblages in research on gender, corporeality and place. In C. A. Taylor & C. Hughes (Eds.), *Posthuman research practices in education* (pp. 168–185). Palgrave Macmillan.

Kaiser, B. M., & Thiele, K. (2014). Diffraction: Onto-epistemology, quantum physics and the critical humanities. *Parallax, 20*(3), 165–167.

Kloetzer, L., Clot, Y., & Quillerou-Grivot, E. (2015). Stimulating dialogue at work: The activity clinic approach to learning and development. In L. Filliettaz & S. Billett (Eds.), *Francophone perspectives of learning through work* (pp. 49–70). Springer.

Kostulski, K., & Kloetzer, L. (2014). Controversy as a developmental tool in cross self-confrontation analysis. *Outlines—Critical Practice Studies, 15*(2), 54–73.

Latour, B. (2002). What is Iconoclash? Or is there a world behind the image wars? In B. Latour & P. Weibel (eds.), *Iconoclash: Beyond the image wars in science, religion and art* (pp. 14–18). The MIT Press.

Latour, B. (2016). Procedure 2: Without the world or within, In B. Latour & C. Leclercq (Eds.), *Reset modernity!* (pp. 91–104). Center for Art and Media.

Laurier, E. (2013). Capturing motion: Video set-ups for driving, cycling and walking, In. P. Adey, D. Bissell, K. Hannam, P. Merriman, & M. Sheller (Eds.), *The Routledge handbook of mobilities* (pp. 493–502). Routledge.

Lee, N. (2001). *Childhood and society: Growing up in an age of uncertainty*. Open University Press.

Lefebvre, H. (1974/1991). *The Production of Space* (D. Nicholson-Smith, Trans.). Blackwell.

Luff, P., & Heath, C. (2012). Some "technical challenges" of video analysis: social actions, objects, material realities and the problems of perspective. *Qualitative Research Journal, 12*(3), 255–279.

Lumsden, K. (2019). *Reflexivity: Theory, method, and practice*. Routledge.

MacBeth, D. (1999). Glances, trances and their relevance for a visual sociology. In P. L. Jalbert (Ed.), *Media studies: Ethnomethodological approaches* (pp. 135–170). University Press of America.

Majchrzak, A., & Markus, M. L. (2012). Technology affordances and constraints in management information systems (MIS). In E. Kessler (Ed.), *Encyclopedia of Management Theory*. Sage.

Mengis, J., Nicolini, D., & Gorli, M. (2018). The video production of space: How different recording practices matter. *Organizational Research Methods, 21*(2), 288–315.
Mesman, J. (2011). Resources of strength: An exnovation of hidden competences to preserve patient safety. In E. Rowley & J. Waring (Eds.), *A socio-cultural perspective on patient safety* (pp. 71–89). Ashgate.
Mesman, J., Walsh, K., Kinsman, L., Ford, K., & Bywaters, D. (2019). Blending video-reflexive ethnography with solution-focused approach: A strengths-based approach to practice improvement in health care. *International Journal of Qualitative Methods, 18*, 1–10.
Milne, E., Mitchell, C., & De Lange, N. (2012). *Handbook of participatory video*. Rowman & Littlefield Publishers.
Mondada, L. (2009). Video recording practices and the reflexive constitution of the interactional order: Some systematic uses of the split-screen technique. *Human Studies, 32*(1), 67–99.
Murris, K., & Bozalek, V. (2019). Diffraction and response-able reading of texts: The relational ontologies of Barad and Deleuze. *International Journal of Qualitative Studies in Education, 32*(7), 872–886.
Pink, S. (2007). Walking with video. *Visual Studies, 22*(3), 240–252.
Stengers, I. (2008). A constructivist reading of process and reality. *Theory, Culture and Society, 25*(4), 91–110.
Stephenson, K. A., Kuismin, A., Putnam, L. L., & Sivunen, A. (2020). Process Studies of Organizational Space. *Academy of Management Annals*. https://doi.org/10.5465/annals.2018.0146.
Thiele, K. (2014). Ethos of diffraction: New paradigms for a (post) humanist ethics. *Parallax, 20*(3), 202–216.
Uprichard, E., & Dawney, L. (2019). Data diffraction: Challenging data integration in mixed methods research. *Journal of Mixed Methods Research, 13*(1), 19–32.
Van der Tuin, I. (2011). A different starting point, a different metaphysics: Reading Bergson and Barad diffractively. *Hypatia, 26*(1), 22–42.
Van der Tuin, I. (2014). Diffraction as a methodology for feminist onto-epistemology: On encountering Chantal Chawaf and posthuman interpellation. *Parallax, 20*(3), 231–244.
Whiting, R., Symon, G., Roby, H., & Chamakiotis, P. (2018). Who's behind the lens? A reflexive analysis of roles in participatory video research. *Organizational Research Methods, 21*(2), 316–340.

CHAPTER 6

Using Video Methods to Uncover the Relational, Interactional and Practical Constitution of Space

Nicolas Bencherki

Abstract Why are visual methods, and in particular video methods, so naturally associated with the study of space in organizational studies? This chapter suggests that this relationship has to do with both video and space having been shown to be *relational* phenomena. Combining work in relational studies of space with French philosopher Gilles Deleuze's writings on moving images allows formulating a communicative approach to the analysis of space using video data, in terms of three sets of relationalities that reflexively fold into one another: (1) the spatial relations more or less faithfully represented in the data; (2) the relations that are outside the data but that made it possible; and (3) the relations defining the observation context.

Keywords Video shadowing · Space · Body · Ethnomethodology · Relationality

N. Bencherki (✉)
Université TÉLUQ, Montréal, QC, Canada
e-mail: Nicolas.Bencherki@teluq.ca

S. Grosjean and F. Matte (eds.), *Organizational Video-Ethnography Revisited*, https://doi.org/10.1007/978-3-030-65551-8_6

6.1 Introduction

Stating that visual methods such as video ethnography are suitable for the study of space may appear commonplace.[1] "Of course," one could say, "we need to see space." Spatiality and visuality appear, indeed, to entertain a special rapport. We view our childhood home on Google Street View and realtors offer 360° virtual visits of apartments. We send our family pictures of charming medieval streets that we wandered during our last trip. It appears that we are not content with an oral description and we do not trust our memory. However, while the connection between space—and geography as its study—and visuality is commonplace, we may find ourselves wondering, "How, exactly, is geography visual?" (Rose 2003). How, indeed, have we come to consider visual methods as a natural means for the study of space and, in particular, why do we rely so much on moving images? Understanding this connection is of special importance to researchers so as to precisely grasp what is gained when using methods such as video ethnography for the study of space.

To understand this relationship, we need to both review our understanding of space and revisit our conception of moving images. While different understandings of space exist, we will adopt a relational view of space that puts at the forefront the tangible embodied and communicative practices through which space is woven (Massey 2003; Rose 1999). Studying space, thus, also means studying these practices. On the other hand, we borrow from the French philosopher Gilles Deleuze (1996) the notion that (moving) images are open-ended systems, being themselves portions of broader systems and made up of many others. These open-ended systems are woven together through communication and they also mobilize the body. What space and moving images share, therefore, is that they are both constituted through the relations between the elements that compose them and to which they give meaning. Those relations are experienced through the body (as noted by Mengis et al. 2018) and may be understood as communicative in nature (Cnossen and Bencherki 2018).

A common approach to understanding these communicative practices analytically draws on ethnomethodology (see Garfinkel 1967). Indeed, ethnomethodology has proven powerful in looking at the spatial arrangement of bodies and other material elements (for instance, queues

[1] I would like to thank François Cooren for allowing me to use, in this chapter, excerpts from data he collected.

in Garfinkel and Livingston 2003; or surgeons' tools and hands in Koschmann and Zemel 2011). Researchers adopting ethnomethodology have regularly used video recordings as a data collection strategy, but also as an analytical tool (Heath and Hindmarsh 2002). However, they have primarily argued in favor of collecting video data because of its ability to keep a "dense" and persistent record of events (Hindmarsh and Llewellyn 2010). They have yet to recognize the parallels in the relational and systemic nature of both video and space.

After discussing this parallel in detail and providing more insight into ethnomethodology's analytical usefulness, this chapter will briefly suggest ways to transcribe video data before delving into an example. The data is drawn from an extensive video shadowing of a building manager in a Manhattan skyscraper, during which a researcher followed the man completing various renovation work. This example will demonstrate how video ethnographic data allows one to observe how people and things relate to one another, and thus compose space. In doing so, it will reveal the key elements of spatial arrangements.

6.2 Space as a Relational Accomplishment

The term "space" has been variously used in organizational studies. It has been used in a metaphorical sense to grant spatial properties to other "things," for instance, "spaces of speech" (Steyaert and Hjorth 2002). On the other hand, the notion of space has also been used in reference to specific locations, such as "cyberspace" or "San Francisco" (Pratt 2002). However, even when using the term "space" in a more literal sense, different understandings of the notion exist. For instance, space has been considered as the distance between two points, as the materialization of power relations and as a lived experience (Taylor and Spicer 2007). Using a distance metaphor, studies have looked, for instance, at how employees may work remotely (e.g., Kociatkiewicz and Kostera 2015), while studies viewing space as the materialization of power have argued that it channels and disciplines bodies (Knox et al. 2008). For its part, viewing space as a lived experience asserts that people constitute space as they give meaning to it, for instance, as they negotiate the relationship between their body, their identity and their workplace (Riach and Wilson 2014). Research on space has also been categorized as either realist, seeking to alter space for organizational needs (Gandini 2015), symbolic, viewing space as a reflection of culture (see the example of a chair in Strati 1996), or critical, viewing space as a territory of power (Shortt 2015).

Despite these different ways of understanding space, there is a growing recognition that space, as physical as it may be, is produced. However, even when agreeing that space is a product, perceptions of how it is produced differ from study to study. In this sense, Wilhoit (2018) distinguishes "space as constructed" in people's meaning of it, from "space as constituted" in their interactions. "Space as constructed" adopts a more phenomenological lens. Studies embracing this approach have relied, for instance, on Henri Lefebvre's triad of space as perceived, conceived and lived (see Michels and Steyaert 2017). In this view, as in Taylor and Spicer's (2007) space as a lived experience, space is (re)produced and evolves as people make sense of it and share, confront and renegotiate those meanings (e.g., Dale 2005; Pepper 2008). What Wilhoit (2018) refers to as the "constitutive" view of space, on the other hand, goes beyond the opposition between meaning and materiality, and views space as anchored in communication and relationality.

This relational view of space is based on the work of human geographers who reject the distinction between space and its experience. Instead, they argue that space is the outcome of practices and that "space is produced as a plenitude of different relations" (Thrift 1999: 310). These authors invite us to think of "such relationalities as performed, as constituted through iteration" (Rose 1999: 247). This does not mean, though, that space is "infinitely plastic," as some forms of space may endure and repeat, thus becoming elements of power (Rose 1999: 248). The plasticity of space is also limited by the fact that every person arriving "here" steps into a "simultaneity of unfinished stories," the traveler's being only one such story among others; as Doreen Massey writes, "If movement is reality itself then what we think of as space is a cut through all those trajectories" (Massey 2003: 107).

What people do, then, also constitutes the space they dwell in and that gives meaning to what they do—but that constitutive process is not reducible to any one activity. Indeed, space is constituted as people position their body respective to one another to form a queue (Garfinkel and Livingston 2003), when they walk and talk together (Mondada 2017) or when they stick together in "viscous" groups that exclude others (Saldanha 2005). People constitute an arts festival by performing in the street with the audience's participation (Munro and Jordan 2013) and a hiking trail by trekking along it (Crevani 2019). Each time, space is constituted and endures thanks to the relative movement of bodies and material elements in collective practices (Cnossen and Bencherki 2018).

6.3 Moving Images as Relational Systems

When wondering what about geography is visual, Rose notes that, while pictures are often used in her discipline as "faithful signs of what was photographed," they also produce "extreme decontextualization" by bracketing out the technical and aesthetic, but also the social, economic and institutional constraints that operate on the object being represented (Rose 2003: 215). For her, though, the solution is not to create better cameras to generate a more faithful representation. Rather, the answer is relational and spatial. As she notes, the relation between the geographer and the photograph—say, of a cup of coffee—is not the same as the relation between her and the cup. When she shows photographs, for instance in a classroom, she becomes an interpreter, translating to her audience what is being seen and gaining authority in the process. The space where the photographs are shown, say a lecture hall, also matters in this relational configuration. This includes the audiovisual equipment within it and that serves to display the photograph, as well as the practical conventions that constitute that space. In this sense, a picture in a gallery, in a café or in a lecture hall is not the same, not because the picture less faithfully represents, say, a cup of coffee, but because the relationship that ties the geographer, the audience and the picture are not the same in each situation. There are, then, at least three sets of relationalities at play: (1) the spatial relations that the photograph represents more or less faithfully; (2) the relations that are outside of the photograph itself but that made it possible, which we can access through the interpretation provided by people or documents that were present at the time (for instance when using visual elicitation techniques; see Shortt 2015); and (3) the relations that define the observation context.

Such a relational understanding is also at play in French philosopher Gilles Deleuze's conception of cinema and moving images (Deleuze 1996). When he discusses the notion of "frame," Deleuze explains this relational nature in systemic terms. For him, "The set cannot divide into parts without qualitatively changing each time: it is neither divisible nor indivisible, but 'dividual' [...] the screen, as the frame of frames, gives a common standard of measurement to things which do not have one"

(Deleuze 1996: 14). The cinematographic image is thus constituted by its parts but also gives them a common meaning as an image. The image, as a system, is open; what is out of the field of vision is not negated but can be made present otherwise by inference or, for instance, through sound (as when a gunshot is heard but not seen). Said otherwise, "Every closed system also communicates" (Deleuze 1996: 16). Indeed, even if the French philosopher was notoriously suspicious of communication, he extensively used the notion of communication to describe how relations between the parts of a frame, including what's outside of the visual frame, are held together.

Relationality and communication are therefore also at play in constituting a (moving) image. Making sense of a picture, then, is not so much a matter of interpretation in the conventional, cognitive sense, as much as it is a matter of accounting for the many relations that are at play in making it what it is (see also the notion of relational aesthetics in Bourriaud 2009). In the same way that Wilhoit (2018) contrasted space as "constructed" and "constituted," we thus see that a relational understanding of images invites us not to consider that an image means whatever signification people invest into it, but to develop a sophisticated apparatus to detect the many trajectories that constitute both space and the images through which it is documented.

In addition to being relationally woven, space and image also share another, related feature: they are both experienced through the body. On the one hand, we perform and occupy space with our bodies (Lewis 1996; Riach and Wilson 2014). On the other hand, photographs and videos are often of our bodies (Hassard et al. 2017) and recorded thanks to our bodies holding the camera, sometimes even putting ourselves at risk (de Rond 2012). Also, both space and images are analyzed through embodied practices, those that are represented in the visual material and those of researchers. Indeed, ultimately, space must be felt, for instance by walking through it (Cnossen et al. 2020), and sight works alongside the researcher's other senses to make up the experience that propels the analysis of visual data (Pink 2006).

6.4 Studying Relationality as a Communicative Accomplishment

Both space and the (moving) images through which we capture it are relationally woven, from the moment the camera seizes space all the way to the lecture hall where it is projected again. The body—the participants' and the researcher's—is a surface on which relations converge and reveal themselves (Matte and Bencherki 2019). In this sense, "the body and embodied conduct is a critical resource for organizational members themselves," as well as for researchers. Yet, the fact is that while research treats the body as a topic of investigation, it mostly continues to use conventional methodologies to do so (Hindmarsh and Pilnick 2007: 1395). There is, therefore, a need for a genuinely communicative and relational perspective that may capture the way bodies reveal the link between visuality and spatiality.

There is indeed growing evidence that relations result from "the work of communication" (Kuhn et al. 2017). However, space and images are not reducible to what people say of them. Communication is also material (Cooren 2018). It is an exchange of symbolic as well as physical action, as when my foot pressing the pedal communicates "go faster" to my car's engine, through mechanical and electronic mediators (Bencherki 2016). Paying attention to how relations are communicatively constituted thus requires an analytical approach that considers communication as social and material action.

Scholars adopting this view look to how space is constituted when things and events that took place there and then act again here and now, thanks to social and material practices that weave together times and spaces (see Vásquez 2016). In this sense, they show that action relates to space through its dislocal character (Cooren and Fairhurst 2008). These researchers borrow ethnomethodology's focus on what people say and do with each other and with their physical surroundings (Garfinkel 1967). This focus is possible thanks to video data (Heath and Hindmarsh 2002), including video ethnography and video shadowing (Meunier and Vásquez 2008; Vásquez et al. 2012), with a strong focus on bodily action, such as cases when a Western humanitarian worker is walking in a Kenyan shantytown (Cooren et al. 2013) or fleeing on muddy roads to take shelter from a possible attack (Matte and Bencherki 2019).

The epistemological status of video-based data is rarely made explicit. The few studies that do refer to it present video as better capturing and recording details that would otherwise escape the researcher's attention (e.g., Sormani et al. 2017). However, visuality is even more intrinsic to ethnomethodology as the approach's core tenet is that people structure their actions so as to make them visible in one way or another (Ball and Smith 2011), drawing attention to the way bodies and materialities are positioned relative to each other and made jointly relevant in people's interactions (Hindmarsh and Heath 2000). Indeed, "the visible bodies of participants provide systematic, changing displays about relevant action" (Goodwin 2004: 157). Through embodied interactional practices, people also position these very practices as relevant to, but also constitutive of, the space they are in (Cnossen and Bencherki 2018).

Ethnomethodologists often review recordings in "data sessions," during which a group of researchers and students collectively watch and comment on recording excerpts. The relational aspect of video data thus also reveals itself through the interactions that surround the viewing and analysis, as data sessions allow insider /outsider collaboration (Bartunek 2008). The researcher who was in the field presents their recordings (first relationality), complements their recordings with statements on what they experienced in the field (second relationality), and their account then confronts the experiences of other data session participants (third relationality). In such settings, video recordings allow one to "inspect, zoom in, juxtapose, annotate and slow down audio-visual records" (Hindmarsh and Tutt 2012: 57). Analyzing video data thus relies on the body as an interpretive engine, especially since analysts also assess the practices they observe by reenacting them (Tutt and Hindmarsh 2011). Around the meeting table or remotely, people's embodied practices make the relations they observe available again for collective scrutiny (Mondada 2007).

However, when writing about spatiality and visuality, there is a risk, in the absence of bodies, of losing the relations that substantiate them. Although it is rarely explicitly addressed, this concern is noticeable in the way ethnomethodological studies write up their analysis and present their video data using different transcription strategies (Jefferson 2004; Mondada 2018). Just as ethnographic writing is an integral part of analysis (Richardson 2000), the presentation of ethnographic data lays out relations between elements and, as what happens during data sessions, invites the reader to inspect, juxtapose or annotate visual elements (Hindmarsh and Tutt 2012). To better preserve the relative movements and actions that take place in the video, the excerpt below inserts speech components directly into the video stills, making these the main vehicle of "transcription" (see Zemel et al. 2019).

6.5 An Illustration: Video Shadowing the Constitution of Space

To illustrate how spatiality and visuality can be analyzed through a relational lens, we draw on recordings from the video shadowing of a building manager in a Manhattan skyscraper, conducted by François Cooren. Shadowing consists of observing the interactions and practices through which a person conducts their daily activities (McDonald 2005). Video shadowing, for its part, supplements this observational work with a video camera (Vásquez et al. 2012). In the excerpt below, the building manager, Eric, discusses, with Edward and Emilio, the air conditioning needs of a tenant business that wants its office separated into two spaces. Figure 6.1 presents six video stills from the video shadowing data along with people's speech during each still. Right before this excerpt started, Emilio fetched a stepladder, positioned it underneath a ceiling tile, and started climbing.

First relationality—the relations that are present in the image: As Emilio climbs up the ladder, the researcher tilts the camera upward to record the ceiling. In the first still, Edward says, "Right here, and then it comes down," and points up, seeming to predict how the duct runs through the suspended ceiling, perhaps to help Emilio decide which ceiling tile to open. However, Emilio, as he climbs up the stepladder, is facing away from Edward and cannot see him, and no one responds to Edward's comment.

Eric then moves toward the researcher's right in the second still, while Emilio opens a ceiling tile, which Edward seems to think is not the right one since he says, "You're on the other side." Again, nobody responds to Edward's comment. Emilio then puts his head inside the opening to look inside the suspended ceiling, twisting his body to the right to look behind him. Meanwhile, Edward moves around the stepladder to the researcher's left and looks up toward the opening. Emilio points his arm in the same direction beneath the ceiling, and says, "Yep, here is where it comes, right here" (still three).

The "yep" seems to indicate that Emilio's visual inspection confirms something that had been said before, perhaps agreeing with Edward's initial comment (although we know that Emilio could not see Edward pointing at the ceiling earlier). In still four, Emilio takes a step down so that his head is no longer in the opening, twists his body to look at Eric (who is out of the frame), points up and says, "Yeah, either the unit's got to go on the room..." (he then says something inaudible).

Fig. 6.1 Stills from the video shadowing data: Emilio climbs up a stepladder

However, Emilio then looks inside the ceiling again, this time toward his left. He seems to see something he had missed the first time as he exclaims, "Oh, oh, I'm wrong! I'm wrong" (still five). He then takes a step down again and points toward the wall behind him, looking at Eric. Without Emilio saying anything, Eric seems to know what he means:

"That's in the other space" (still six). Following this sequence, everyone moves to the other space.

A detailed analysis of what we see in the video highlights the importance of body positioning in weaving relations between people and space. How Emilio, Edward and Eric position themselves with respect to one another, and how one of them has his head in the ceiling, clarifies who spoke to whom, who knows what, and what made Emilio recognize that he was wrong.

Second relationality—the relations that are absent but make a difference: François Cooren is the researcher holding the camera. He experienced and felt the relations at play, on and off the frame. François followed Eric for three days as he visited tenants in their premises, went up and down elevators, and moved around the building. Being familiar with Eric's work, François knew that Edward ran a HVAC business, Emilio being one of his technicians. Eric was thus their client. However, François witnessed that they knew each other well, for instance when Eric, earlier that day, seemed sincerely concerned about Edward having hurt his finger on his way to their meeting, and when the three men exchanged family anecdotes in the elevator. François also noted that they worked in a similar manner in several premises, showing they were used to working together. Typically, Eric would explain what the tenant business wanted, Emilio would inspect the premises and suggest how to do it, and Edward would take notes and discuss resources. On their way from the elevator to the room in the excerpt, Eric had explained the work being done on that floor and they passed by the other space, which used to be part of the same large room.

The researcher's presence in the field thus provides access to otherwise absent relations that allow one to revisit the original analysis. For instance, it may seem rude that Emilio turned his back on Edward and ignored what he said. However, knowing that the two men were used to working together, and that it was Emilio's role to inspect premises, implies that Edward's statement was a mere suggestion. Also, we may have been surprised that Eric understood that the duct came from the other room when Emilio pointed at the wall, but less so when we realize that the group had passed by the other space, which is behind the wall. In each of these instances, other relations, absent from the video frame, overlay the first and alter their meaning.

Third relationality—the relations in the observation situation: Visible relations take on another meaning when they are embedded in the larger set of relations that the researcher experienced. However, this embedding takes place, in its turn, in yet other relations that define the situation during which the observation takes place. In this case, while François recorded the data, I wrote the chapter. I did not experience the space and bodies we were looking at, while he had. Although data sessions normally involve several people looking at a screen together, in our case, due to the 2020 coronavirus pandemic, we held a data session through videoconferencing with just the two of us, to discuss the spatial implications of the excerpt while each viewing the video on our own computer. This analytical situation led to a particular distribution of roles between us and generated ideas that would have been different in a conventional data session. We had already held data sessions previously to look at other parts of the video shadowing data from which the excerpt is drawn (e.g., Bencherki 2014), but my limited familiarity still led me to play the part of the outsider, with François as the insider.

This role duality meant that our joint analysis took a question/response format. I expressed surprise at some of what occurred during the interaction and François offered clarification or helped me work things out. For instance, I drew François' attention to Emilio's apparent neglect of Edward's comments. It was my surprised reaction that led him to tell me that the men had worked together and known each other for a while. When I asked how François seemed to anticipate that Emilio would open a ceiling tile when he tilted the camera upward, he pointed out that the three men were already intently looking upward and told me that he had observed the three men complete the same routine before. It is my own perplexity that enabled François to determine which relations mattered or not in the scene, which in turn helped me to write the previous section.

6.6 Discussion: Learning About Space Through Video Shadowing

What does the above video shadowing data tell us that would have been different otherwise? First, to reiterate the theory reviewed earlier, and in agreement with ethnomethodologists and geographers alike, we learn about how people and things relate to each other, and the importance of bodies in revealing those relations. For instance, the crucial element of the situation—Emilio climbing up a stepladder and opening the ceiling—is never mentioned in speech. Yet, its effect is manifested both in the others' movements as they repositioned themselves to look at it, and in the researcher's body, as he tilted the camera so that the ceiling occupied most of the visible frame. The participants' and researcher's bodily position also matters as there was no verbal reference to the fact that Emilio turned toward Eric (i.e., out of frame at the researcher's right) and spoke to him in still four. From words alone, we could interpret that he was responding to Edward's remarks in stills one and two. Again, Eric's statement in still six, "That's in the other space," would not make sense without understanding the bodily and relational configuration of the space.

In addition, our analysis shows how the black square in the middle of the screen, where Emilio hid his head, is a materialization of his special epistemic stance, again in agreement with prior work on embodied (and, arguably, spatial) knowledge (Hindmarsh and Pilnick 2007; O'Connor 2005). The subject of the video shadowing, Eric, was left out of the picture, leaving Emilio at the center and thus making the researcher complicit in recognizing that being up on the stepladder provided him a privileged perspective. This is never mentioned verbally and, if we focused only, for instance, on the fact that Edward was Emilio's hierarchical superior, or that Eric was their client, we would not expect Emilio to lead the interaction as he did. Video data clarifies that it was his relation to space that granted him an authoritative viewpoint.

Second, and relatedly, we extend literature on the body's role in understanding space (Hindmarsh and Pilnick 2007; Pink 2006) to clarify that analysis of video shadowing and space must include all three relationalities that we introduced above. While resisting the urge to draw too quickly on outside context to account for what occurs in an interaction, our analytical strategy shows that surprising elements of the video data can result in shifts to "higher" sets of relations. It is, therefore, breakdowns in the ability to rely on in-frame data that materialize or make salient the effects of out-of-frame relations. This is true of what Emilio saw in the opening, to which we do not have access, but is partly witnessable in what he said and did afterward. This is consistent with Massey's (2003) theory that we always step into "unfinished stories" and into trajectories that began before we got here and will continue beyond this particular relational encounter. Our bodies, as they move while contributing to a continued sense of selfhood, also weave together a seemingly smooth fabric of space from loose strings of experience.

Finally, to continue on a textile metaphor and use the terminology of Deleuze (1993), the three sets of relationalities fold into one another.

This fold, more precisely, consists of the reflexive thinking and the gaze that each set casts upon the previous. Relationality, indeed, is an exercise in reflexive embodied empathy (Finlay 2005). In the first relationality, the participants themselves appeared to have a bodily understanding of each other's movements and of the space they were in, as they knew how they would feel and move themselves if they were in each other's place. In the second relationality, François was able to recall what he saw and felt while present in the field, and was therefore able to be empathetic with his past self and with other participants. Finally, in the third relationality, the conversations that François and I had related to how I would have behaved in similar circumstances, and my surprise that the participants did not do so. In the latter case, reflexive embodied empathy is congruent with the idea that data sessions involve "reenactment" (Tutt and Hindmarsh 2011). Through successive layers of reflexivity and embodiment, relationalities fold into each other, generating analysis that does not abstract the relational nature of reality, but rather recapitulates it, preserving the fullness of experience throughout.

Our original question was: Why are spatiality and visuality so tightly related? Why, more specifically, is video shadowing so appropriate to the study of space? We can now answer that it is because video allows us to see more of space, but also because space and images alike are relationally constituted. Further, it is because bodies—the participants' and the researcher's—provide reflexive access to the successive layers of relationalities that, in turn, allow the analysis of space. The message, then, is that researchers should preserve the thread that ties together the relational richness of each stage as they transform their data from observation, to recording, and then to text. Another lesson is to remain attentive to the researchers' own relational entanglements, which are integral to analysis.

References

Ball, M., & Smith, G. (2011). Ethnomethodology and the visual: Practices of looking, visualization, and embodied action. In E. Margolis & L. Pauwels (Eds.), *The SAGE handbook of visual research methods* (pp. 392–413). Sage.

Bartunek, J. M. (2008). Insider/outsider team research: The development of the approach and its meanings. In A. B. Bashni, N. Adler, S. A. Mohrman, W. A. Pasmore, & B. Stymne (Eds.), *Handbook of collaborative management research* (pp. 73–92). Sage.

Bencherki, N. (2014). L'ethnométhodologie et l'École de Montréal. In H. Bourdeloie & D. Douyère (Eds.), *Méthodes de recherche sur l'information et la communication* (pp. 141–166). Mare et Martin.

Bencherki, N. (2016). How things make things do things with words, or how to pay attention to what things have to say. *Communication Research and Practice, 2*(3), 272–289.

Bourriaud, N. (2009). *Relational aesthetics*. Presses du réel.

Cnossen, B., & Bencherki, N. (2018). The role of space in the emergence and endurance of organizing: How independent workers and material assemblages constitute organizations. *Human Relations, 72*(6), 1057–1080.

Cnossen, B., de Vaujany, F. X., & Haefliger, S. (2020). The Street and Organization Studies. *Organization Studies*. https://doi.org/10.1177/0170840620918380.

Cooren, F. (2018). Materializing communication: Making the case for a relational ontology. *Journal of Communication, 68*(2), 278–288.

Cooren, F., & Fairhurst, G. T. (2008). Dislocation and stabilization: How to scale up from interactions to organization. In L. L. Putnam & A. M. Nicotera (Eds.), *The communicative constitution of organization: Centering organizational communication* (pp. 117–152). Lawrence Erlbaum Associates.

Cooren, F., Matte, F., Benoit-Barné, C., & Brummans, B. H. J. M. (2013). Communication as ventriloquism: A grounded-in-action approach to the study of organizational tensions. *Communication Monographs, 80*(3), 255–277.

Crevani, L. (2019). Organizational presence and place: Sociomaterial place work in the Swedish outdoor industry. *Management Learning, 50*(4), 389–408.

Dale, K. (2005). Building a social materiality: Spatial and embodied politics in organizational control. *Organization, 12*(5), 649–678.

de Rond, M. (2012). Soldier, surgeon, photographer, fly: Fieldwork beyond the comfort zone. *Strategic Organization, 10*(3), 256–262.

Deleuze, G. (1993). *The Fold: Leibniz and the Baroque*. University of Minnesota Press.

Deleuze, G. (1996). *Cinema 1: The movement-image*. University of Minnesota Press.

Finlay, L. (2005). "Reflexive embodied empathy": A phenomenology of participant-researcher intersubjectivity. *The Humanistic Psychologist, 33*(4), 271–292.

Gandini, A. (2015). The rise of coworking spaces: A literature review. *Ephemera, 15*(1), 193–205.

Garfinkel, H. (1967). *Studies in ethnomethodology*. Prentice-Hall.

Garfinkel, H., & Livingston, E. (2003). Phenomenal field properties of order in formatted queues and their neglected standing in the current situation of inquiry. *Visual Studies, 18*(1), 21–28.

Goodwin, C. (2004). Practices of seeing visual analysis: An ethnomethodological approach. In T. Van Leeuwen & C. Jewitt (Eds.), *The handbook of visual analysis* (pp. 157–182). Sage.

Hassard, J., Burns, D., Hyde, P., & Burns, J.-P. (2017). A visual turn for organizational ethnography: Embodying the subject in video-based research. *Organization Studies*. https://doi.org/0170840617727782.

Heath, C., & Hindmarsh, J. (2002). Analysing Interaction: Video, ethnography and situated conduct. In T. May (Ed.), *Qualitative research in practice* (pp. 99–121). Sage.

Hindmarsh, J., & Heath, C. (2000). Embodied reference: A study of deixis in workplace interaction. *Journal of Pragmatics, 32*(12), 1855–1878.

Hindmarsh, J., & Llewellyn, N. (2010). Finding organisation in detail: Methodological orientations. In N. Llewellyn & J. Hindmarsh (Eds.), *Organisation, interaction and practice: Studies of ethnomethodology and conversation analysis* (pp. 24–46). Cambride University Press.

Hindmarsh, J., & Pilnick, A. (2007). Knowing bodies at work: Embodiment and ephemeral teamwork in anaesthesia. *Organization Studies, 28*(9), 1395–1416.

Hindmarsh, J., & Tutt, D. (2012). Video in analytic practice. In S. Pink (Ed.), *Advances in visual methodology* (pp. 57–73). Sage.

Jefferson, G. (2004). Glossary of transcript symbols with an introduction. In G. H. Lerner (Ed.), *Conversation Analysis: Studies from the first generation* (pp. 13–31). John Benjamins.

Knox, H., O'Doherty, D., Vurdubakis, T., & Westrup, C. (2008). Enacting airports: Space, movement and modes of ordering. *Organization, 15*(6), 869–888.

Kociatkiewicz, J., & Kostera, M. (2015). Into the Labyrinth: Tales of Organizational Nomadism. *Organization Studies, 36*(1), 55–71.

Koschmann, T., & Zemel, A. (2011). "So that's the ureter": The informal logic of discovering work. *Ethnographic Studies, 12*, 31–46.

Kuhn, T., Ashcraft, K. L., & Cooren, F. (2017). *The work of communication: Relational perspectives on working and organizing in contemporary capitalism*. Routledge.

Lewis, C. (1996). Woman, body, space: Rio Carnival and the politics of performance. *Gender, Place & Culture, 3*(1), 23–42.

Massey, D. (2003). Some times of space. In S. May (Ed.), *Olafur Eliasson: The weather project* (Vol. 1–The Unilever Series). Tate Modern. http://weboeliasson.dyndns.info:8080/PDF/Some_times_of_space.pdf.

Matte, F., & Bencherki, N. (2019). Being followed by an organization: A hauntological perspective on organizational ethnography. In F. Malbois & F. Cooren (Eds.), *Methodological and ontological principles of observation and analysis: Following and analyzing things and beings in our everyday world* (pp. 202–232). Routledge.

McDonald, S. (2005). Studying actions in context: A qualitative shadowing method for organizational research. *Qualitative Research, 5*(4), 455–473.

Mengis, J., Nicolini, D., & Gorli, M. (2018). The video production of space: How different recording practices matter. *Organizational Research Methods, 21*(2), 288–315.

Meunier, D., & Vásquez, C. (2008). On shadowing the hybrid character of actions: A communicational approach. *Communication Methods and Measures, 2*(3), 167–192.

Michels, C., & Steyaert, C. (2017). By accident and by design: Composing affective atmospheres in an urban art intervention. *Organization, 24*(1), 79–104.

Mondada, L. (2007). Operating together through videoconference: Members' procedures for accomplishing a common space of action. In S. Hester & D. Francis (Eds.), *Orders of ordinary action: Respecifying sociological knowledge* (pp. 51–67). Routledge.

Mondada, L. (2017). Walking and talking together: Questions/answers and mobile participation in guided visits. *Social Science Information, 56*(2), 220–253.

Mondada, L. (2018). Multiple temporalities of language and body in interaction: Challenges for transcribing multimodality. *Research on Language and Social Interaction, 51*(1), 85–106.

Munro, I., & Jordan, S. (2013). 'Living Space' at the Edinburgh Festival Fringe: Spatial tactics and the politics of smooth space. *Human Relations, 66*(11), 1497–1525.

O'Connor, E. (2005). Embodied knowledge: The experience of meaning and the struggle towards proficiency in glassblowing. *Ethnography, 6*(2), 183–204.

Pepper, G. L. (2008). The physical organization as equivocal message. *Journal of Applied Communication Research, 36*(3), 318–338.

Pink, S. (2006). *The future of visual anthropology: Engaging the senses*. Routledge.

Pratt, A. C. (2002). Hot jobs in cool places. The material cultures of new media product spaces: The case of south of the market, San Francisco. Information, *Communication & Society, 5*(1), 27–50.

Riach, K., & Wilson, F. (2014). Bodyspace at the pub: Sexual orientations and organizational space. *Organization, 21*(3), 329–345.

Richardson, L. (2000). Writing: A method of inquiry. In Y. S. Lincoln & N. K. Denzin (Eds.), *Handbook of qualitative research* (pp. 923–948). Sage.

Rose, G. (1999). Performing space. In D. Massey, J. Allen, & P. Sarre (Eds.), *Human geography today* (pp. 247–259). Polity Press.

Rose, G. (2003). On the need to ask how, exactly, is geography "visual"? *Antipode, 35*(2), 212–221.

Saldanha, A. (2005). Vision and viscosity in Goa's psychedelic trance scene. *ACME: An International Journal for Critical Geographies, 4*(2), 172–193.

Shortt, H. (2015). Liminality, space and the importance of 'transitory dwelling places' at work. *Human Relations, 68*(4), 633–658.

Sormani, P., Alač, M., Bovet, A., & Greiffenhagen, C. (2017). Ethnomethodology, video analysis, and STS. In U. Felt, R. Fouché, C. A. Miller, & L. Smtih-Doerr (Eds.), *The handbook of science and technology studies* (4th ed., pp. 113–138). MIT Press.

Steyaert, C., & Hjorth, D. (2002). 'Thou Art a Scholar, Speak to it...'—On Spaces of Speech: A Script. *Human Relations, 55*(7), 767–797.

Strati, A. (1996). Organizations viewed through the lens of aesthetics. *Organization, 3*(2), 209–218.

Taylor, S., & Spicer, A. (2007). Time for space: A narrative review of research on organizational spaces. *International Journal of Management Reviews, 9*(4), 325–346.

Thrift, N. (1999). Steps to an ecology of place. In D. Massey, J. Allen, & P. Sarre (Eds.), *Human geography today* (pp. 295–322). Polity Press.

Tutt, D., & Hindmarsh, J. (2011). Reenactments at work: Demonstrating conduct in data sessions. *Research on Language and Social Interaction, 44*(3), 211–236.

Vásquez, C. (2016). A spatial grammar of organising: Studying the communicative constitution of organizational spaces. *Communication Research and Practice, 2*(3), 351–377.

Vásquez, C., Brummans, B. H. J. M., & Groleau, C. (2012). Notes from the field on organizational shadowing as framing. *Qualitative Research in Organizations and Management: an International Journal, 7*(2), 144–165.

Wilhoit, E. D. (2018). Space, place, and the communicative constitution of organizations: A constitutive model of organizational space. *Communication Theory, 28*(3), 311–331.

Zemel, A., Hebenstreit, B., & Koschmann, T. (2019, May). *Glossing practices during surgical instruction in the operating room.* 69th annual conference of the International Communication Association, Washington, DC.

CHAPTER 7

Participant Viewpoint Ethnography and Mobile Organizing

Elizabeth Wilhoit Larson

Abstract This chapter describes participant viewpoint ethnography (PVE), a video research method. PVE involves two components. First, a participant uses a wearable camera to create a video from their perspective of some activity. Second, the researcher watches the video with the participant and interviews the participant about the video. This method is useful for helping participants attend to aspects of their experience that may be innate and difficult to verbalize and gives the researcher better understanding of the embodied aspects of activities. The method is illustrated with an example from the author's research on bike commuters and future research directions for using PVE to study mobilities in organizations are suggested.

Keywords Participant viewpoint ethnography · Space · Sensory data · Embodied experiences · Mobility

E. Wilhoit Larson (✉)
Auburn University, Auburn, AL, USA
e-mail: elarson@auburn.edu

S. Grosjean and F. Matte (eds.), *Organizational Video-Ethnography Revisited*, https://doi.org/10.1007/978-3-030-65551-8_7

7.1 Introduction

In this chapter, I detail participant viewpoint ethnography (PVE), a method in which participants wear a camera to capture a mobile and spatial phenomena and then watch their video with the researcher to narrate and elaborate on the experience (Wilhoit 2017c; Wilhoit and Kisselburgh 2016). Because the video moves with the participant, it captures the participant's trajectory (Massey 2005) and allows the traces of an ephemeral, mobile path to emerge (Spinney 2011). In viewing this path, one can then see the other trajectories that come into contact with this mobile path, creating space and allowing the object of study to emerge through the method. PVE also contains a reflexive component as participants narrate their experience and reflect on the path that was created through the video.

As I will demonstrate through examples from my research on bike commuters, PVE is a useful method for studying mobile aspects of organizing that other methods might struggle to capture. In studying bike commuters, I sought to understand how they were present in the space of the road and interacted with cars and pedestrians. I was curious about how they moved through space and moved between surfaces (e.g., road, sidewalk, grass) to create a path. I wanted to see how cyclists created and claimed space when there were not designated spaces for cyclists. All of these questions would be difficult to study though a retrospective method like interviews because they involve so many quick transitions and interactions that bike commuters themselves might only be implicitly aware of. Traditional ethnography would also be challenging as it is difficult to take field notes or remember what has happened when you are trying to follow someone on bike. Given the limitations of other methods, I developed PVE to better study this mobile phenomenon.

In this chapter, I will begin by discussing other visual research methods that provided inspiration for PVE. I will then describe the method of PVE in detail with examples from my research. Additionally, I am an organizational communication scholar and my goals in studying bike commuters were both to understand the organization of transportation as well as transitions between work and home. Given this interest, I conclude the chapter by suggesting other areas of mobile organizing that could be further studied through the use of PVE.

7.2 Visual Research Methods

Photography as a research tool is not new; anthropologists have long taken photos to capture ethnographic data (Pink 2014). However, first disposable cameras (see Clark-Ibáñez 2004), then digital and cellphone photography have made visual research easier to conduct and have led to an increased interest in using photos and videos in research (see Margolis and Pauwels 2011). Although there are many existing visual research methods that use images in ways that align with a range of epistemologies and research paradigms (Meyer et al. 2013), I will focus here on one method (photo-elicitation interviews) that was a particular inspiration for PVE.

In PEI, photographs are used as a shared anchor (Harper 2002) or "medium of communication" (Clark-Ibáñez 2004: 1512) between the researcher and interviewee. Photos can be taken by participants (e.g., Clark-Ibáñez 2004; Collier and Collier 1986) or by the researcher (e.g., Harper 1987). During the interview, photographs are a common frame of reference and the researcher asks questions based on the images. Scholars have found various advantages of PEI including increased rapport, less participant fatigue, more detailed responses, the ability to ask better questions of participants, new sources of meaning creation through participant-taken images, and accessing knowledge that participants might have trouble articulating (Buchanan 2001; Clark-Ibáñez 2004; Collier and Collier 1986; Harper 2002; Lapenta 2011; Wilhoit 2017c). PEI was an influential method for the development of PVE, as PVE uses participant-created videos as the basis for an interview.

7.3 Research Context

I developed PVE for a project studying bike commuters (people who ride bikes to work) in a university town in the American Midwest, where riding bikes to work is not a normal form of transportation. My initial goal for this project was to understand how bike commuters were publicly performing an alternative practice, both in the road and at their organizations. In order to understand these experiences, I realized that I would need a method that went beyond only interviews or observations. Interviews would tell me what bike commuters thought of their experiences, but would not give me any outside perspective of how others might interact with them. Similarly, observations would allow me to understand what it was like to negotiate traffic or enter one's workplace flushed and sweaty, but without understanding the meaning participants assigned to these activities. I wanted to be able to both have a glimpse into participants' activities and have a sense of how participants understood these activities. Additionally, doing observations of mobile activities presents some logistical challenges (Spinney 2006, 2011). Although I was comfortable on a bike, the idea of trying to following someone else through traffic while somehow taking field notes did not seem appealing. Given these limitations of existing methods for answering the questions I set out to answer, I developed a new method, participant viewpoint ethnography, that is ideal for understanding mobile organizing phenomena (see Wilhoit 2017c; Wilhoit and Kisselburgh 2016). In the next section, I describe the method in-depth using examples from the study described here.

7.4 Participant Viewpoint Ethnography

For this project, I began data collection with semi-structured interviews conducted with bike commuters in the two adjoining towns I was studying ($n = 40$). In the first round of interviews, I asked questions about bike commuters' routes to work, interactions with car drivers, pedestrians, and other cyclists, their reasons for biking to work, their co-workers' reactions to their transportation choices, and their transitions into and out of work and home on bike. Following these initial interviews, I sampled participants for the PVE phase of this project from the participants with whom I conducted the first round of interviews. The purpose of using PVE in addition to more traditional interviewing was to gain additional reflexive and phenomenological data (see van Manen 1990) to better understand the lived experience of bike commuting. Phenomenological methods aim to give the researcher more direct contact with the phenomenon they are studying while also acknowledging that it is usually difficult for people to articulate their own experiences (Husserl 1931). Phenomenological methods therefore use various tools (often writing) to help participants direct their attention toward and articulate their lived experience (Moustakas 1994; van Manen 1990).

PVE therefore consists of two stages: collecting video data from the perspective of participants and conducting a reflexive interview with participants. As mentioned, for the first phase of PVE in this study, I recruited participants from a larger sample of bike commuters. At the end of first-round interviews, I asked participants if they would be interested in continuing their participation. Participants who also completed the second and third rounds of the research were given a gift certificate to a local bike shop as compensation. Out of 40 participants for the first round of interviews, five participated in the PVE phase of research. For the first phase of PVE, participants were given a GoPro camera, which is a rugged video camera with a wide-angle lens designed for recording action sports. The camera comes with a variety of mounts for different sports, including a head strap. Participants used the head strap to wear the camera on either their head or bicycle helmet to record their journey to and from work from their perspective. Participants were instructed to begin recording before they left home and to stop recording once they had arrived at work in order to capture the transitions out of home and into work on bicycle. Additionally, participants were instructed to stop recording if they encountered a sensitive situation like entering a restroom to change clothes or a prolonged conversation with a colleague. However, no such situations arose in data collection. In total, participants recorded 10 videos (five going to work, five coming home from work) that totaled 185 minutes of video footage. Individual videos ranged from four to 34 minutes.

After participants recorded the videos, I watched the videos to identify any specific aspects of the videos about which I was curious or wanted more clarification. Based on whichever video I found more interesting or had more questions about, I chose one video from each participant to review with them. I then met with each participant to conduct a follow-up interview, the second stage of PVE. During the follow-up interview, I watched the chosen video together with the participant. I asked participants to comment on aspects of their commute like the choices they made, the route they took, interactions with others, and the transitions between work and home. I also asked questions at points as we watched the videos. In many cases, we also would pause or rewind the videos to allow for more detailed discussion of specific moments. This method then reflects the dialogical approach to visual research, in which visuals offer a means for starting a conversation with an organizational member with the goal of understanding how the participant interprets imagery based on their experiences (Meyer et al. 2013).

Following the interview portion of PVE, I coded the videos. My goal in analyzing the videos on their own was to understand what was going on and to gain insight into the activity and organization of bicycle commuting. At this level then, I was taking more of an archaeological approach (Meyer et al. 2013), seeking to reconstruct the meanings and activities in the video. To understand the videos from this perspective, I used a sequential (Knoblauch and Schnettler 2012) and emergent coding process (Charmaz 2003). I watched the videos several times, noting general themes and categories of events, objects, and activities present in the videos. I then reviewed the videos again, watching for a specific category each time, generating lists of time-stamped notes of relevant moments and aspects for each category. The major categories coded for were surfaces (i.e., what surfaces did a cyclist ride on?), interactions and intersections, material artifacts, office transitions, and home transitions.

In addition to analyzing the videos, I also analyzed the PVE interviews from watching the videos with participants. For the initial analysis of those videos, I coded them along with the first, larger set of interviews I did for the project, using iterative analysis (Tracy 2013). Then, following independent analysis of the videos (trying to make sense of what was happening from an external perspective) and the interviews (trying to understand how participants understand and experience biking to work), I was able to look at the two perspectives together. Looking at these two sets of data combined provided several insights. First, I was able to enrich interview data with sensory data. In the videos, I could hear participants breathing hard as they biked uphill and see how they navigated difficult intersections, creating a richer account of their embodied experiences (Ellingson 2017). Second, I was able to see when there were differences between how participants understood their commute and what the videos demonstrated. For example, Chase said that he thought he biked on the road for 75% of his commute. However, analysis of his video showed that he changed surfaces 21 times in the four minutes it took him to ride his bike to work. Third, the combination of these two methods allowed me to understand both what participants did and how they made sense of that activity. The videos gave me perspective on participants' movements and behavior, but the interviews helped me to see how participants understood their own activity and why they made certain choices. For example, the videos often gave a sense of vulnerability of bikes in the road with cars speeding by. Some participants felt this vulnerability and described the choices they made to uphold their safety. Other participants did not feel vulnerable and explained their more aggressive biking styles in light of their confidence in cycling.

Although the method is most useful in situations when a participant is able to give reflections on their experience, it is also important to note that the researcher can be the one doing the reflecting. In a follow-up study on cyclists in Copenhagen (Wilhoit 2017a), I was unable to recruit participants to participate in PVE. However, part of my goal of that research was to understand how the cycling affordances of Copenhagen communicated and my experience as an outsider learning how to read the physical cycling environment was a valuable one. As part of my research, I would bike with the GoPro, making recordings of my own biking experiences. I would then review the videos, taking note of not only what happened as recorded in the videos, but also how I felt and my thought process behind navigating certain situations. The researcher can therefore also be a valuable PVE participant, depending on the research context.

In general, PVE has two major methodological advantages: gathering reflexive, phenomenological data (Wilhoit and Kisselburgh 2016) and creating more communication with participants (Wilhoit 2017c). First, phenomenological approaches to research value the individual experience and understanding phenomena through a close focus on how an individual experiences and understands the world (van Manen 1990). PVE did just that for this project. For example, one aspect of the bike commute that I wanted to understand were transitions in and out of the workplace on bicycle. Because participants continued to wear the camera until they were in their office or workspace, I was able to see how participants came into work and then discuss these routines in detail with participants learning why and how they maintained these routines. Even though I had asked about these transitions in the initial interviews, they did not have nearly the same depth or detail because participants did not have a record of what they generally did to spur conversation. This leads to the second major advantage of PVE (and many other dialogical visual methods) that PVE leads to new and additional forms of communication in the research context (Wilhoit 2017c). The videos helped participants to talk about parts of their experience that were either so innate and tacit they were not aware of them or that participants did not know how to articulate otherwise. The videos also helped me as a researcher to communicate and ask questions that might not have occurred to me as important in a regular interview. For instance, all of the PVE participants had very specific routines involving bike racks and where they preferred to lock up their bikes. In the PVE interviews, I was able to ask more questions about these routines and generate more participant reflections as a result of having imagery as a shared anchor (Harper 2002).

7.5 Evaluation of PVE for Studying Mobile Organizing

PVE has been a very useful method for my research on bike commuters. It has provided me with valuable data that I would have had trouble accessing otherwise. In this section, I consider the advantages of PVE specifically for studying mobile organizing. In the final section, I suggest possibilities for PVE in ongoing mobile organizing research.

The first advantage of PVE for studying mobility is that movement can be difficult to capture and studying it from the perspective of those moving was useful for understanding both what they did and how they experienced it. My study of bike commuters demonstrated that only talking to participants was not sufficient for fully understanding their experiences. For instance, one topic that I was interested in understanding was communication between cyclists and car drivers and how the two groups negotiated shared road space. Although I asked participants about this in my initial interviews, their descriptions of this experience were somewhat limited, as talk makes it difficult to capture all of the tacit embodied experiences that take place in such an encounter. However, in the PVE videos, I was able to see cyclists repeatedly turning their head to look over their shoulder for oncoming traffic in a way that indicated some of the stress and fragility of being a cyclist in a space generally designated for cars. In many cases, understanding mobility is about more than just knowing that someone went from location A to location B, but understanding the journey and transitions are also important. Logistically, it would have been difficult to follow and carefully observe cyclists, but through participant viewpoint videos, I was able to collect data not only on a trajectory, but also the experience of that trajectory.

Second, PVE is useful for understanding the spatial aspects of mobility. Movement necessarily involves space and my use of PVE gave me some new insights into how cyclists construct space (Wilhoit and Kisselburgh 2015, 2017). First, in research on space, the experiential and socially constructed aspects of space can conflict with the objective aspects of space. These two understandings of space are often seen in conflict with each other (Wilhoit 2016). However, through PVE, both the participant narrative and experience as well as the (still-constructed) reality of the video are both valuable for understanding the creation of organizational space through mobile organizing practices. One of the major findings of my research was that cyclists are participating in collective action, even though many cyclists do not have direct interaction with each other (which is normally a requirement for collective action). I made this argument based on the many layers of space that cyclists create in terms of their routes, space on the road, bike path, or sidewalk, and experience. Again, I was able to understand space in a multifaceted way that went beyond just paths to work or car driver versus cyclist conflicts. Similarly, for other mobilities research, PVE can be used to understand both how space is constructed through movement as well as how space is constructed through meaning-making processes (Wilhoit 2018).

Third, Massey (2005) has defined space as a coming together of multiple trajectories in which sometimes unexpected connections are made and other connections which seemed inevitable are deconstructed. PVE is also ideal for capturing moments of ephemeral trajectories coming together to better understand the construction of space. Again, a perhaps obvious bundling of trajectories, but one that PVE allowed me to more fully investigate, was the connection between bikes and cars on the road. The relationship between cars as dominant and bikes as marginalized in the space of the road became an important finding of my study (Wilhoit and Kisselburgh 2017). Although I had some insights into this relationship from my initial interviews, the moments in the videos that showed cyclists in conflict with cars and my conversations with participants that suggested they felt vulnerable in those moments helped me to better understand the nature of these transportation spaces. Both of these ways of better studying the construction of space through PVE fit with the goal of mobilities research to deconstruct space as static and understand its shifting and constructed nature (Sheller and Urry 2006).

Finally, PVE is useful for mobility research because it allows scholars to attend to embodied and sensory aspects of activity. Embodiment is a foundational area of theory for mobilities research and there is a need for research that re-centers the body and its abilities to sense place (Sheller and Urry 2006). As mentioned in the previous section, PVE helped me to better understand the embodied experience of cyclists. I conducted the PVE interviews in late fall and was able to see participants putting on layers of clothing as they prepared to go to work (several participants looked in a mirror to ensure that the camera was recording before leaving home and I was able to see their attire). I heard participants heavy breathing and the strain on their bicycles as they pedaled up steep hills. I saw them frantically looking over their shoulders as they tried to make it across traffic to turn left. I got a glimpse of the joy of coasting quickly down a steep hill. There were many embodied, sensory experiences that I was able to glimpse and then further understand through the PVE interviews that would be difficult to capture in a standard qualitative interview. Again, these data offer a new understanding of spaces and mobility.

7.6 Future Directions in Mobile Organizing Research and PVE

Although bike commuters are an obvious example of organizational mobility, organizations are increasingly on the move in other, perhaps more subtle ways (Kuhn et al. 2017), as organizations change more quickly, workers change organizations more often, and people, goods, and information move around the globe to accomplish organizational goals. I suggest that PVE and similar methods offer researchers new tools for better understanding the shifting, moving, and constructed world of work today. To conclude, I discuss a few areas for future organizational mobilities research and how a method like PVE might be useful for gaining new insights into these organizing phenomena.

First, PVE could be used to study other forms of commuting and work-life transitions. There is research that suggests that commuting can be a positive time of transition between work and home for many workers (Ory et al. 2004; Páez and Whalen 2010; Wilhoit 2017b). PVE could be used to better understand which aspects of the commute workers find beneficial and which aspects are stressful as well as seeing how workers more generally make sense of their commute in terms of both these positive and negative aspects. By recording a journey to or from work and then reviewing and discussing that video with a researcher, a worker might better be able to elucidate the value of commuting and the specific moments and aspects that help with relaxation, role transition, and autonomy.

Second, I suggest that PVE could be used to better understand how individual workers with spatial flexibility create, use, and make sense of varied workspaces. Individual workers are increasingly mobile with the ability to work from home or third spaces, whether or not they are self or organizationally employed. Understanding how workers make use of third spaces like coffee shops and coworking spaces is still an emerging area of research (Constantinescu and Devisch 2018; Garrett et al. 2017; Spinuzzi 2012). There are many aspects of working in third spaces that are yet to be studied and that could be considered through the use of PVE. For example, anecdotally, it seems that many workers who utilize third spaces move between spaces throughout the day. Using PVE to understand these transitions could be useful—how and when do workers move between spaces? How do they create and then disassemble the personal space that they create within third spaces while they are working? PVE could also be used to understand how workers actually use and understand spaces like coworking spaces—recording workers' viewpoints on actually doing work and capturing distractions, interactions, and movements and then interviewing workers about those videos to further understand their use of spaces.

These examples demonstrate the potential of PVE for ongoing mobilities research, allowing scholars to attend to the shifting constructions of space and meaning as experienced by participants. Through its combination of observation and reflection, PVE is well-suited to projects that require a new perspective on organizing.

References

Barada, V. (2013). Sarah J. Tracy, Qualitative research methods: Collecting evidence, crafting analysis, communicating impact. *Revija Za Sociologiju, 43*(1), 99–101.

Buchanan, D. A. (2001). The role of photography in organization research: A reengineering case illustration. *Journal of Management Inquiry, 10*, 151–164.

Charmaz, K. (2003). Grounded theory: Objectivist and constructivist methods. In J. A. Holstein & J. F. Gubrium (Eds.), *Inside interviewing: New lenses, new concerns* (pp. 509–535). Sage.

Clark-Ibáñez, M. (2004). Framing the social world with photo-elicitation interviews. *American Behavioral Scientist, 47*, 1507–1527.

Collier, J., & Collier, M. (1986). *Visual anthropology: Photography as a research method*. University of New Mexico Press.

Constantinescu, T. I., & Devisch, O. (2018). Portraits of work: Mapping emerging coworking dynamics. *Information Communication and Society, 21*(9), 1263–1278.

Ellingson, L. L. (2017). *Embodiment in qualitative research*. Routledge.

Garrett, L. E., Spreitzer, G. M., & Bacevice, P. A. (2017). Co-constructing a sense of community at work: The emergence of community in coworking spaces. *Organization Studies, 38*, 821–842.

Harper, D. (1987). *Working knowledge: Skill and community in a small shop.* University of Chicago Press.
Harper, D. (2002). Talking about pictures: A case for photo elicitation. *Visual Studies, 17,* 13–26.
Husserl, E. (1931). *Ideas: General introduction to pure phenomenology.* Macmillan.
Knoblauch, H., & Schnettler, B. (2012). Videography: Analysing video data as a "focused" ethnographic and hermeneutical exercise. *Qualitative Research, 12,* 334–356.
Kuhn, T. R., Ashcraft, K. L., & Cooren, F. (2017). T*he work of communication: Relational perspectives on working and organizing in contemporary capitalism.* Routledge.
Lapenta, F. (2011). Some theoretical and methodological views on photo-elicitation. In E. Margolis & L. Pauwels (Eds.), *The Sage Handbook of Visual Research Methods* (pp. 201–213). Sage.
Margolis, E., & Pauwels, L. (Eds.). (2011). *The Sage handbook of visual research methods.* Sage.
Massey, D. (2005). *For space.* Sage.
Meyer, R. E., Höllerer, M. A., Jancsary, D., & van Leeuwen, T. (2013). The visual dimension in organizing, organization, and organization research: Core ideas, current developments, and promising avenues. *Academy of Management Annals*, *7*(1), 489–555.
Moustakas, C. E. (1994). *Phenomenological research methods.* Sage.
Ory, D. T., Mokhtarian, P. L., Redmond, L. S., Salomon, I., Collantes, G. O., & Choo, S. (2004). When is commuting desirable to the individual? *Growth and Change, 35,* 334–359.
Páez, A., & Whalen, K. (2010). Enjoyment of commute: A comparison of different transportation modes. *Transportation Research Part a: Policy and Practice, 44*(7), 537–549.
Pink, S. (2014). *Doing visual ethnography* (3rd ed.). Sage.
Sheller, M., & Urry, J. (2006). The new mobilities paradigm. *Environment and Planning a, 38*(2), 207–226.
Spinney, J. (2006). A place of sense: A kinaesthetic ethnography of cyclists on Mont Ventoux. *Environment and Planning D, Society and Space, 24*(5), 709–732.
Spinney, J. (2011). A chance to catch a breath: Using mobile video ethnography in cycling research. *Mobilities, 6,* 161–182.
Spinuzzi, C. (2012). Working alone together: Coworking as emergent collaborative activity. *Journal of Business and Technical Communication, 26,* 399–441.
van Manen, M. (1990). *Researching lived experience: Human science for an action sensitive pedagogy.* State University of New York Press.

Wilhoit, E. D. (2016). Organizational space and place beyond container or construction: Exploring workspace in the communicative constitution of organizations. *Annals of the International Communication Association, 40,* 247–275.

Wilhoit, E. D. (2017a). Affordances as material communication: How the spatial environment communicates to organize cyclists in Copenhagen, Denmark. *Western Journal of Communication.* https://doi.org/10.1080/10570314.2017.1306098.

Wilhoit, E. D. (2017b). 'My drive is my sacred time': Commuting as routine liminality. *Culture and Organization.* https://doi.org/10.1080/14759551.2017.1341518.

Wilhoit, E. D. (2017c). Photo and video methods in organizational and managerial communication research. *Management Communication Quarterly, 31,* 447–466.

Wilhoit, E. D. (2018). Space, place, and the communicative constitution of organizations: A constitutive model of organizational space. *Communication Theory.* https://doi.org/10.1093/ct/qty007.

Wilhoit, E. D., & Kisselburgh, L. G. (2015). Collective action without organization: The material constitution of bike commuters as collective. *Organization Studies, 36,* 573–592.

Wilhoit, E. D., & Kisselburgh, L. G. (2016). Through the eyes of the participant: Making connections between researcher and subject with participant viewpoint ethnography. *Field Methods, 28,* 208–226.

Wilhoit, E. D., & Kisselburgh, L. G. (2017). The relational ontology of resistance: Hybridity, ventriloquism, and materiality in the production of bike commuting as resistance. *Organization.* https://doi.org/10.1177/1350508417723719.

PART III

“Outsider” and “Insider” Video-Ethnographer: Exploring Multimodal and Multisensorial Workplace Settings

CHAPTER 8

Doing Video Ethnography Research with Top Management Teams

Feng Liu, Michael Jarrett, and Linda Rouleau

Abstract This chapter draws on our own journeys and on other studies in searching for and developing appropriate methods by which to study top management team strategic decision-making in meetings in real time. After introducing video-based approaches in organizational research, the chapter proposes three ways of including research participants' perspectives into our interpretations to close the gap between "insider" and "outsider" views of the research process and outcomes. We call these methodological approaches: refining, distributive, and holistic. These

F. Liu (✉)
Saint Mary's University, Halifax, NS, Canada
e-mail: Feng.liu@smu.ca

M. Jarrett
INSEAD (European Institute of Business Administration), Singapore, Singapore
e-mail: michael.jarrett@insead.edu

L. Rouleau
HEC Montréal, Montréal, QC, Canada
e-mail: linda.rouleau@hec.ca

S. Grosjean and F. Matte (eds.), *Organizational Video-Ethnography Revisited*, https://doi.org/10.1007/978-3-030-65551-8_8

approaches will be presented and evaluated based on selected video episodes from the authors' and other studies. The chapter concludes with a final discussion, including implications for research and practice.

Keywords Top management · Multimodal · Emotions · Embodied experiences · Sense-making

8.1 Introduction

Top management teams are said to be the most important teams in any organization because they make critical decisions and strategic choices that further influence an organization's performance (e.g., Finkelstein et al. 2009; Goodstein et al. 1994; Knight et al. 1999; Liu et al. 2018; Liu and Maitlis 2014; Wiersema and Bantel 1992). Research suggests that the characteristics of top management team members, what they think and do, and how they interact with each other significantly influence the processes and outcomes of strategic decision-making (Hambrick and Mason 1984). However, most of these studies examine these strategic choices and interactions via coarse proxies, such as team members' demographic factors, and functional and educational backgrounds, to indicate the kinds of interactions and explain how they influence the processes and outcomes of TMT decision-making (e.g., Baysinger et al. 1991; Finkelstein et al. 2009; Hill and Snell 1988; Wiersema and Bantel 1992). As a result, the findings from this stream of research on organizational outcomes based on demographics of TMT members have yielded both mixed and confusing results (Cannella et al. 2008; Hambrick et al. 2015; Pitcher and Smith 2001). Thus, it prompts an increasing interest in opening up the "black-box" of TMTs so as to examine exactly how members interact with each other when making strategic decisions (Carpenter et al. 2004; Hambrick 2007).

Therefore, we have seen attempts, including our own, to identify finer and more appropriate methods to examine the interactions, as well as to respond to calls to narrow the gap between management scholarship and practice. These include observations and interviews to explore the TMT member interactions when they make strategic decisions for the organizations (e.g., Beech and Johnson 2005; Kisfalvi and Pitcher 2003; Kisfalvi et al. 2016; Maitlis and Lawrence 2003) focusing on what TMT members say and do. However, not until most recently have researchers started looking into these interactions with the new technology of portable video cameras using the method of video ethnography (e.g., Jarrett and Liu 2018; Liu and Maitlis 2014). Such methods can be used either from an Etic (outsider) or Emic (insider) view. In this paper, we propose to look at these interactions through an integrated view. Based on video episodes from our own and others' research, we propose three ways of integrating both perspectives.

To develop our argument, the chapter will briefly recast the emergence and benefits of video-based approaches to organizational research. It will examine the case to include respondents' perspectives in our interpretations and understanding of organizational phenomena as we try to close the gap between the "insider" and "outsider" views of the research process and outcomes. These approaches will be presented and evaluated based on selected video episodes from the authors' and other studies. The chapter concludes with a final discussion, including implications for research and practice.

8.2 Video Ethnography: What Is It?

Video recording has been used in education, medicine, communication, and language research for decades (e.g., Andersen and Adamsen 2001; Armstrong and Curran 2006; Goodwin 1994; Heath and Hindmarsh 2002; Iedema et al. 2009; Pink et al. 2017) but it is a relatively new method in organization and management research. In other words, it is an established research method finding a new home. Video work provides an "ethnographic turn" to new forms of ethnography among organizational scholars (Rouleau et al. 2014). It is also gaining acceptance within the business community for design thinking, marketing studies, and understanding customer-staff interaction in companies such as Unilever, GlaxoSmithKline, and Intel (Poyner 2008). Increasing interest is fostered by technological advances, smaller and more sophisticated video cameras, smartphones, and changes in social attitudes reflected by the YouTube generation and social media.

The application of video ethnography to organization and management research is adding more and more new insights to our understanding of organizations (Christianson 2018; Gylfe et al. 2016; Jarrett and Liu 2018; LeBaron et al. 2018). It is a "multimodal" method, that is, it pays attention to the combination of different modes, such as talk, gestures, gazes, tools, movements, and so on, that are used in concert to produce meaning (Streeck et al. 2011). Therefore, it provides exceptional opportunities to examine how gestures, bodies, spaces, documents and artifacts are deployed in, for example, strategizing and organizing activities (e.g., Gylfe et al. 2016; Jarzabkowski et al. 2015) and enriches our understanding of strategy and organization in ways that go beyond previous works focusing only on strategists' talk.

For example, using video ethnography to study TMT strategic decision-making has several advantages. First, video recording is a superb tool to capture micro-expressions, or nuanced and rich emotional expression cues from facial/vocal/verbal/body movement channels when they occur. Video recording significantly enhances the quality of the data captured because "it provides infinitely rich detail of transient events" (Cohen 2010: 34), which is beyond any researcher's ability to capture (Jarrett and Liu 2018; Liu and Maitlis 2014).

Second, video recording captures participants' actions and emotion expressions in vivo (Goodwin 1994), which is not possible using other methods, such as surveys or interviews, by which researchers collect participants' recollections of emotions they experienced in the past (e.g., Huy's series of studies on emotion and organizational change). In vivo capture further eliminates the bias of post hoc justification by participants for their particular actions and emotions because of social desirability (Leonard-Barton 1990; Vaara et al. 2004; Vardaman et al. 2010).

Third, video recording facilitates later data analysis. This method keeps a faithful, permanent record of the data long after the fieldwork is finished and allows repeated scrutiny of important episodes during the data analysis stage, since the data can be analyzed, reanalyzed, reviewed, and shared by many researchers (Armstrong and Curran 2006). This is especially important in our case because we have been working as teams on multiple top management and board team video recording projects. Due to constraint of resources, only one team member typically travels to the research site, collects data, and then, later, the team works together to analyze the data. Team members who were not on site will have access to faithful and live recording of the TMT meeting data. This direct access reduces other team members' reliance on the focal team member's notes and interpretations of what was going on in TMT meetings. Thus, it provides an additional validity check.

8.3 "Etic" and "Emic": Crossing the Divide

8.3.1 "Etic" vs. "Emic" Approaches to Research

The origins of the Emic/Etic distinction in linguistics can be traced back to Pike (1967), who distinguished between phonemic and phonetic accounts of the sounds of language. As originally formulated, "phonemic accounts are member-relevant rules about the sound contrasts of language that native speakers have inside their heads, while phonetic accounts are researcher-relevant distinctions about how these sounds are observably realized by native speakers" (Markee 2013: 1). In qualitative organization studies, an Etic approach means interpreting data from the researcher's view; while an Emic approach means developing empathy with, and giving voice to, participants, that is, to understand the researched phenomenon from the participant's point of view (Morris et al. 1999) (Table 8.1).

These two are often presented as different approaches to understanding how knowledge is created by the researcher and the research participants. The spectrum runs from objective, measurable criteria-based experiments, to surveys, to "going local" in field studies, to participant involvement in the collection and interpretation of data (Finlay 2002). However, we share the view that in practice the Emic/Etic contrast is a continuum rather than a dichotomy, and that they could be integrated, thereby creating synergy (see Cheung et al. 2011; Gover et al. 2016; Morris et al. 1999).[1] One way of integrating is to incorporate participants' interpretations to help researchers confront, modify, and hone their own interpretations (e.g., Finlay 2002; Jarrett and Liu 2018; Smith 1994). This is how Emic insights might refine Etic explanations. We call this the "refining" approach and will use the data from the Liu and Maitlis (2014) study to illustrate how this approach could be used in a relatively short and smaller-scale research program in which the research team interviewed the participants, and viewed excerpts of video-recorded meetings with them at the end of the research project.

Another way of integrating the Etic and Emic approaches is to establish a mutually enriching relationship between the researcher and the research participants in a longitudinal research design. Through longer immersion

[1] There are strong advocates for both separate as well as integrated approaches. See Cheung et al. (2011), Headland et al. (1990), Morris et al. (1999), and Walsh et al. (2007) for further discussion.

Table 8.1 Assumptions of Etic and Emic perspectives

	Research goals/orientation	*Methods (data gathering and analysis)*	*Benefits and drawbacks (selective examples)*	*Epistemology (the nature of knowledge)*
Etic/Outside view	Describe/predict causal relationships and variance between established constructs, test hypotheses. Orientation: Positivist approach	External observable & measurable features, large numbers, comparative, "objective," e.g., survey[a]	Benefits: Equivalence & comparability; identifies variance among units of analysis; statistical equivalence; clear answers by testing hypotheses; "impartiality" Drawbacks: Cultural/insider insensitivity; imposed theory; incremental contributions to theory	Knowledge is produced by the researcher "second order" meaning
Emic/Inside view	Understand the "inner world" of context, patterns, temporality and relationships between actors and system as a whole. Elicits meaning Orientation: Constructivist approach	Ethnographic, long-standing involvement, small numbers e.g. case(s), elicit "view from participants," reflexive dialogue	Benefits: Captures a broadened experience of "reality"; culturally sensitive; context incorporated into design; indigenization of research process; relevance; fosters sense-making Drawbacks: local biases; concerns of "rigor"; particularization of the context	Knowledge is produced and co-created in collaboration with the participants

(continued)

Table 8.1 (continued)

	Research goals/orientation	*Methods (data gathering and analysis)*	*Benefits and drawbacks (selective examples)*	*Epistemology (the nature of knowledge)*
Integrated Etic-Emic view	Understand and integrate the perspective of the research participants and the researcher. Orientation: Complementarity	Application of both methods. The emphasis can be different for different types of studies, by sequencing or by key stages of a study, e.g., Emic exploratory to begin and test later in a mixed-methods approach. More sophisticated approach ensures a constant interplay between the Etic and Emic	Benefits: Bridge the divide between theory and experience; create new synergies e.g. abductive theorizing; helps delineate between general and particular context; provides insights into what (Etic) and why (Emic) Drawbacks: integrating research paradigms; demanding to pull mixed-methods data together and present in succinct manner	Knowledge is produced and integrated by both the respondent & researcher—"double hermeneutic." Meaning is co-constructed

[a]Although typical of this approach, qualitative methods using interviews and observation can also fall within an Etic approach. Similarly, quantification of observation data can also be used when taking an Emic approach.

in the field, and more frequent contact, the researcher could not only fine-tune his/her interpretation of what's going on with the participants' input but could also bring this information into later data collection as that which merits further examination. Furthermore, the participants are more aware of their own behaviors. We call this the "distributive" approach and select an excerpt from Jarrett and Liu (2018), to illustrate.

Finally, we present excerpts from additional studies (Lahlou 2011; Smets et al. 2011, 2015) that "democratize" the research process and engage research participants in more meaningful ways, ranging from data collection to interpreting results, which we call the "holistic approach".

The range of Etic-Emic approaches to video ethnography is wide and varied in complexity and scope. However, the common element is that they all seek to incorporate the contextual-insider's view into the meaning-making of the research. Thus, the decision researchers make will depend upon matters such as the study's purpose, research question, resource availability, as well as context. In highlighting different approaches, we selected the three we mentioned above: the "refining" approach, the "distributive" approach, and the "holistic" approach.

8.3.2 The Refining Approach

We see this approach as shorter in duration (a few months), with fewer observations of interactions, and with respondent participation providing a refinement to researcher's insights. In Liu and Maitlis (2014), the authors state: "In keeping with the extant literature on emotion and strategizing, our interest is in individuals' displayed emotions, rather than their intra-psychic states" (p. 203). Additionally, the authors say: "we decided to ground our analysis primarily in the observational data (the video/audio recordings and transcripts of the meetings)" (p. 212). Nevertheless, one of the authors did interview each of the team members at the end of the observation period. She also revisited certain excerpts of the video-recorded meetings with the TMT members in order to understand their perspectives on what occurred during them, and on participants' feelings.

We now use one excerpt from Liu and Maitlis (2014) to explain how the participant's knowledge was used to inform the researchers' interpretations of what was going on in the video-recorded meetings. The research setting was a company that produced video games. This excerpt is from a TMT discussion of a new HR strategy to manage the sharp reduction of staffing that occurs at the end of the game production cycle, or employee "roll-off." Victor, one of the TMT members, did not think the new strategy would work well for his game team; thus, he sought help from other team members to find a better solution (selected from Liu and Maitlis 2014: 219–220).

Victor:	If Michael doesn't want to go to [game team 4], he doesn't really have a choice. You know, like that's – we're going to sell it to him: 'They asked for you, blah blah?' I'm sure, I'm pretty confident he's going to get excited and really want to do it. But let's use him as a case study for a second and say, OK, he says no. There's no other roll-out – I come to you guys, there's no other role – what the hell do we do? [Excited]
Simon:	So, then there are not many choices for him. [Neutral]
Charlie:	Would you like a job still? [Amused]
Victor:	(Gives examples with two of his team members). What is the result? Is the result, literally, 'well you know you don't really have much of a choice', or 'your choice is there's no job for you or you take this'. And can we say that? [Excited]
Simon:	To be safe, you go: 'look, this is where the company needs you right now. You know, we need your skills on this project; you're the man to do the job. Obviously, we're going to try to accommodate you as much as possible. There's two options, go to either one of these. But if it's the one – that's where we need you right now.' [Excited]
	...
Kathy:	... so it's a bit of a gap-filler and there's something else cool coming down the road. So, it's a bit of a carrot for people. [Neutral]
Victor:	We can sell them that we hope there's a carrot. Even now, I can't ... [Frustrated]
	...
Victor:	I can't even tell them if we're doing [game name], or whatever it's called. [Frustrated]
John:	On Monday I had announced that originally, we were doing [game name]. [Neutral]
Victor:	Yesterday you asked them, 'Are we going to do it or not?' [Annoyed]

Focusing only on this excerpt, an outsider might be surprised to see a senior team member becoming more and more frustrated when discussing headcount issues. However, during the interviews, in which one author watched important excerpts with team members, and during this author's long immersion in the field, when she gained insight from the participants, the authors were informed that headcount fluctuation is one of the most critical issues in the game industry. In addition, the then on-going acquisition negotiation caused uncertainty as to which games were next to be produced. As a result, Victor could not tell his team members that their expertise was not needed for the current game in production, but that it might be for the next game in line. Victor was further frustrated that keeping an employee on his team in the absence of a task to be accomplished would hurt the team's profit.

Thus the participants' perspectives helped the authors to refine and enrich their understanding of what they observed in the video-recorded meeting, that is, why a senior TMT member became frustrated and annoyed when the team discussed headcount issues.

8.3.3 The Distributive Approach

This approach is longitudinal but divided into several shorter and focused bursts of video data collection over a longer period; thus the term "distributive". It is focused ethnography in orientation as the researcher works in situ, not only recording and conducting interviews, but also engaging through informal observations, discussions, and direct experiences of the "local" context. While interpretative, it is not a full ethnographic approach. However, it affords ethnographic-orientated researchers an opportunity to establish a mutually enriching relationship and to meet two other purposes: (i) it provides a sense of the typical meaning of the actions they are observing, and (ii) it allows the recovery of the (typical) knowledge of the actors in context (Knoblauch and Schnettler 2012: 345). It captures what Goffman (1983) called the "interaction order", meaning it is situated within a particular context embedded in the interactions.

The research context for this study is a global services company, and the episode involves the TMT's discussion of strategic digital marketing and whom to appoint. The whole team is present, but the main dialogue is between the CEO and a Managing Director. A quiet but non-verbal participant is the Sales & Marketing Director (SMD) (selected from Jarrett and Liu 2018: 372). It was the embodied interactions that were the focus of this study (Gylfe et al. 2016; Streeck et al. 2011). That is, how did the actors' talk and movement—gaze, orientation, gestures and posture—affect TMT outcomes?

Managing Director (MD):	This to me (looking at the Sales & Marketing Director), is possibly one of the most important hires (pauses) in the entire business. (CEO shifts orientation and looks at MD)
MD:	(continues) I think in the entire organization, if you think about roles. (CEO adjusts himself in his seat to face MD directly)
MD:	I think this is incredibly important, this role… incredibly important (voice tales off).
CEO:	And what's the implication of that? (snappy response) (Looks directly at MD, and uses hand gesture pointing at the MD)
MD:	(sits back) I don't know, (hand gesture toward CEO) … you've had time to think about it.
CEO:	I have (snappy response, direct eye contact, active chopping hand gesturing toward MD) …and I've taken a decision about it!
SMD:	ha: ha: ha: ha: ha: ha: haha: ha: ha (Turns to look at CEO)
MD:	I took a sharp intake of breath when you said, er, Chris, (pauses) so when I, I, er, I read the (pre-meeting briefing) papers I didn't see anything about Chris. I was just thinking, wow, this is an incredibly important role. You best get it right; that was what I was thinking (long pause). Hmm. I have no idea, hence my question (with active hand gestures) … how easy is it going to be to find someone out there…

CEO:	(interrupts and over talks MD) It's not … (it's) very difficult.
MD:	(Er) I think Chris's got some skills …but … (pauses) rr:: (long pause)
CEO:	Well, you just got to trust my judgment on this.
SMD:	The positive thing is…
CEO:	(interrupts) Let's not discuss this anymore. It's a decision! (and touches SMD on the arm)
SMD:	No no (okay) … (and touches the CEO on the shoulder)
CEO:	And I think Chris will do an outstanding job. I really do. CEO goes on to say how Chris is right for the job and concludes that part of the meeting.

The episode depicts an interaction between the CEO and his direct report, the Managing Director. Most people quickly observe that the discussion represents a disagreement of perspectives between the two and, with their non-verbal cues, a source of potential conflict. The MD does not directly confront his boss, but constantly questions the assumed validity of the proposed hire's qualities to fit the job. However, the interaction shortly comes to a close with the CEO declaring: "It's a decision". The CEO uses his power of role authority and legitimacy over more subtle influence tactics. The MD withdraws. He appears annoyed and uncomfortable (Etic view).

However, other information, insights, and realities existed that as researchers we would not have gleaned without the respondents' discussion in viewing themselves on video in situ. For example, when the MD watched the video, he reported that he was resentful and frustrated, not so much with the outcome, but with his recognition that the SMD and CEO had built an alliance, and how this alliance often played to his disadvantage. We see this in the embodied expression of the two toward the end of the episode. He continued to describe the depth of his negative feelings toward SMD, but in the formal meetings these emotions were never expressed. Along with similar new information from each of the three players in the episode, we as researchers were able to discern implicit, repetitive patterns, and to develop new insights into the psychological and inner dynamics of this particular TMT that were not apparent without an Emic view (see Jarrett and Liu 2018).

In summary, "Video recordings are only tools. The analytical focus lies on the interaction taking place in a certain social situation. Making sense of what has been tape-recorded essentially depends upon additional contextual knowledge" (Knoblauch and Schnettler 2012: 335). This insight is afforded by a distributive and focused ethnography.

8.3.4 The Holistic Approach

The principles of this Etic-Emic approach rest on proximal relationships rather than on distal, greater duration, collaborative data collection methods, interpretations that are co-constructed, and complexity to weave Etic and Emic interplays. For example, the study by Morris et al. (1999), on personality across cultures illustrate a holistic model of Etic-Emic based on constant comparison and mutual refinements of each, leading to an integrated, "dual perspective" of the phenomena under study.

With regard to organizations, few if any studies cover the entire spectrum of a holistic approach. However, there are several that do take key aspects. For instance, Lahlou (2011), illustrates a workplace ethnography that provides a dual perspective. First, the study innovates methodologically by using two types of cameras: one a video that captures a classic viewpoint of the action (outside/Etic view) and one for the participant, who wears a light "subcam" on the head to get their view (insider/Emic). To our knowledge, this approach has not been used in TMT research; however, we believe it provides TMT researchers with a good tool resulting in new research insights. We should be aware that, in education and communication research, there have been emerging interests in using Google glasses in video ethnographic work (e.g., Due 2015; Paterson and Glass 2015, 2020), which is similar to the subcam used in the Lahlou study, from which TMT researchers could learn (Fig. 8.1).

Secondly, the study features not only collaborative data capture, but also reflexive collaboration between participant and researcher in making sense of the footage. Lahlou captures the dialogue and draws the reader's attention to the collaborative nature of them reviewing the video (Lahlou 2011: 622–623) (see transcript below). Thirdly, the author concludes: "While discussing the interpretation with the subject is not new, we found

Fig. 8.1 Same scene taken from a traditional camera (left) and a subcam (right) (from Lahlou 2011: 616)

that adopting an 'evidence-based' approach, by discussing a material that strongly supports recall of subjective states (intentions, emotions…) brought ground-breaking progress to our research" (p. 624).

The extract illustrates the dialogue between the researcher and a participant, who is a specialist trouble-shooter of computer problems. They have reviewed the video footage together and are now collectively sense-making (selected from Lahlou 2011: 622–623).

Subcamer:	But that's a very unusual case I mean. With most of, stuff, you know, ahmm it's a pretty automated process, I could give somebody a piece of paper and they could follow the process and get rid of like 90% of the stuff. Hm. This was a particularly awkward one.
Researcher:	It's interesting, because you had to display hmm a lot of strategy.
Subcamer:	Yeah, well more than anything you know you've got to show a bit of initiative as well, ahm, and, you know often you'd start going on Google or something like that to find the answers and… You know with a lot of problem-solving with computers, you know, probably like, I'd say, maybe 50% of it is prior knowledge and then 50% of it is knowing where to go to find the answers. You know.
Researcher:	I see

Subcamer:	Like here, you know, with the guys that work here [they are expected] to know to find the answers. Hmm. You know. That, that's, You know, I joke with my Mom about it. My Mom will say 'Well how do I fix it?' So I say 'Google it!' You know, because that's what I'm gonna do, y'know [laughs]. You know. That, that's how you fix lot of these problems.
Researcher:	So, so, there's a moment when, ehm, just ehm. Well. It's like first you, you thought that could be a, you saw very quickly that was not a classic case, right, because the guy [already
Subcamer:	[yeah
Researcher:	had taken the virus [away
Subcamer:	[yeah
Researcher:	which means that he he's computer-literate also
Subcamer:	Yeah, exactly. He'd, he'd actually done, you know, probably the first two steps that we would have done here, so we were already at an advanced … place
Researcher:	All right. So then you check that he did right
Subcamer:	Exactly
Researcher:	And then you realize that this is gonna be a tougher case than expected?
Subcamer:	Yeah

Smets et al.'s (2011, 2015) study also provides a rich description of their year-long ethnographic, multi-site, team-based approach to video ethnography in a reinsurance company. The authors provide detailed examples of their challenges. These include capturing interactions across multiple events and sites within the organization, which can entail continuous access negotiation for each stage of the study. Sometimes, permission is gained to film video interactions on the spot and some people tend to share less when videoed. In addition, team co-ordination and logistic issues, such as following brokers around, where to place the equipment, and managing the overall project in a coherent manner added to the complexity of the study.

However, these challenges also generated opportunities for learning, in which researchers shared lessons on methodological insights for the "fieldwork", "headwork", and "textwork" of ethnography (Van Maanen 2011). For example, the use of multi-site teams addressed issues of being in the field (work). In making sense of the data (headwork), the teams benefited by reviewing each other's material and getting a different insider-outsider perspective of the researcher who was on site and the one who was not, providing additional insight. The research team also developed protocols to share themes from their field work on a regular basis. Finally, research outputs (textwork) follow headwork. Multi-teams provided richness in the writing and presentation of the final output (Smets et al. 2015). Material can also be appropriately shared, with research participants, at academic conferences and with practitioners, where pictures may convey more than words. These may be met with challenges of the researchers' interpretation, but this can only improve the quality of the process and outputs, which most researchers would welcome (Table 8.2).

8.4 Conclusion

This brief chapter provides insights into the role and value of video ethnography as a method to study, understand, and theorize the micro-behaviors within organizations using top management teams in particular. It opens up the "Black Box" (Hambrick 2007) and reveals hidden realities to the researcher. It further illustrates that video-ethnographic methods provide rich details of interactions. It is a source of validation for data analysis and provides new insights not available from traditional approaches alone. Moreover, the chapter extends our understanding and application of video methods by teasing out the distinction between Etic and Emic approaches to research. In the former, the researcher's external view provides objectivity, measurement, and generalizability; whereas the latter provides meaning, contextual insights, another form of validity, and opportunities for theorizing.

Both approaches have their benefits and drawbacks (see Table 8.1). However, we have argued for an integrated approach of Etic-Emic that gains the benefits of each while mitigating their drawbacks. Nevertheless, in making these choices, the usual criteria of good research apply: What is the purpose of the study? What design would follow? How might the methods help answer our research question? What stages of the research program suggest which approach to use when? How do we integrate our findings and report our results? We do not suggest that crossing the boundary between Etic and Emic is a simple step, but believe that

Table 8.2 Degrees of integration in Etic-Emic studies

Type of study	*Key features of study*[a]	*Context of research*	*New data from this approach*	*Key insights*
"Refining" approach (see Liu and Maitlis 2014; Armstrong and Curran 2006)	Shorter term; fewer video observations, analysis grounded in video recordings but views clips with participants during interviews at the end of the study	Short video-ethnographic study of a TMT in their strategizing process	Foregrounds felt emotions in addition to emotional expressions; participants' perspectives on the video-recorded interactions	Richer and enhanced understanding of video-recorded TMT interactions
"Distributive" approach (see Jarrett and Liu 2018; Knoblauch and Schnettler 2012)	Longitudinal but divided into short, focused sessions over several events; context matters; involvement of participants in final stage of interpretation of data; Etic incorporating Emic experience and revisions	Video, interviews, observations over multiple events. Examining TMT & their board interactions over a year and their decision-making.	The approach elicited new information about participants' motivations, felt emotions, surfaced implicit bias and reflexive learning	Conceptualization of new intragroup, psychological mechanisms as well as a "novel approach" to video methods
"Holistic" approach (see Lahlou 2011; Morris et al. 1999; Smets et al. 2011)	Ethnographic, long term and evolving; High level of participant involvement; Strong interplay between Etic and Emic	Examining practices across cultures; the practice work within an insurance setting; the work of service technicians	Develop joint new knowledge, understanding and practice	Dual perspective, transfer research into practice

[a]Time (intensity), level of participant involvement; research design/methodological complexity

exploring these different perspectives leads to better and more insightful research outcomes.

The benefits of an integrated Etic-Emic approach to research have already been developed in other fields of social science, including personality research, cross-cultural studies, and justice judgments. These ideas have also been recently applied in different ways to organizational studies, where we identified a spectrum of integrated approaches: "refined", "distributive" and "holistic". These represent the types we found in our research and those of our colleagues, and we recognize that they are neither comprehensive nor ideal. However, based on our studies, we illustrate some of the benefits as well as the implications for research and management practice of using video ethnography taking an Integrated Etic-Emic approach.

There are several implications for research. The use of an integrated approach can provide new information that the researcher(s) alone might not elicit. For example, in the second study, researchers reviewing the video material with the respondents elicited new and surprising information concerning their motivations and emotions. Furthermore, the use of this process of reflexive dialogue with respondents (Finlay 2002) provides novel insights both for the respondents themselves, their role in the top management team, as well as the dynamics of the TMT. Moreover, these additional insights created the conditions for abductive theorizing—provided by the surprising result that emerged from the process—and additional interpretations of the interactions within these TMTs. The novelty that arises provides the opportunity for new theory (Lahlou 2011; LeBaron et al. 2018). Finally, the integrated approach also provides better context validity and strikes a balance between research rigor and management relevance.

The research process also provides opportunities for management practice. For instance, TMT members reported that the viewing and discussion of themselves from the video recordings provided a non-threatening form of feedback. As one executive put it: "It was seeing myself in context" that was a major trigger for learning. This was stated even though many of the TMT members reported having received executive coaching at some point in their careers and did not gain these insights. Thus, in situ video feedback provides opportunities for management learning, leadership development, and team effectiveness.

Using an Etic-Emic approach also narrows the gap between theory and practice, rigor and relevance, and insiders and outsiders. As Gover et al. (2016), conclude: "Findings that reveal individuals' perspectives of the culture change process are likely to aid researchers and practitioners in their attempts to comprehend how to introduce cultural change in a manner that is likely to be accepted by organizational members" (p. 578).

These lessons from the field provide opportunities to extend the boundaries of our research questions and our study design, resulting in insights that will further enhance knowledge, and develop practice.

Acknowledgements The author(s) disclosed receipt of the following financial support for the research, authorship, and/or publication of this article: We gratefully acknowledge the support of the Social Science and Humanities Research Council of Canada (Grant # IDG 430-2017-00529) and the INSEAD R&D Committee and the INSEAD Alumni Fund.

References

Andersen, C., & Adamsen, L. (2001). Continuous video recording: A new clinical research tool for studying the nursing care of cancer patients. *Journal of Advanced Nursing, 35*, 257–267.

Armstrong, V., & Curran, W. (2006). Developing a collaborative model of research using digital video. *Computers & Education, 46*, 336–347.

Baysinger, B. D., Kosnik, R. D., & Turk, T. A. (1991). Effects of board and ownership structure on corporate R&D strategy. *Academy of Management Journal, 34*(1), 205–214.

Beech, N., & Johnson, P. (2005). Discourses of disrupted identities in the practice of strategic change. *Journal of Organizational Change Management, 18*(1), 31–47.

Cannella, A. A., Jr., Park, J. H., & Lee, H. U. (2008). Top management team functional background diversity and firm performance: Examining the roles of team member colocation and environmental uncertainty. *Academy of Management Journal, 51*(4), 768–784.

Carpenter, M. A., Geletkanycz, M. A., & Sanders, W. G. (2004). Upper echelons research revisited: Antecedents, elements, and consequences of top management team composition. *Journal of Management, 30*(6), 749–778.

Cheung, F. M., van de Vijver, F. J., & Leong, F. T. (2011). Toward a new approach to the study of personality in culture. *American Psychologist, 66*(7), 593–603.

Christianson, M. K. (2018). Mapping the terrain: The use of video-based research in top-tier organizational journals. *Organizational Research Methods, 21*(2), 261–287.

Cohen, A. J. (2010). Audiovisual recording. In A. J. Mills, G. Durepos, & E. Wiebe (Eds.), *The Sage encyclopaedia of case study research* (pp. 32–34). Sage.

Due, B. L. (2015). The social construction of a Glasshole: Google Glass and multiactivity in social interaction. *PsychNology Journal, 13*(2), 149–178.

Finkelstein, S., Cannella, S. F. B., Hambrick, D. C., & Cannella, A. A. (2009). *Strategic leadership: Theory and research on executives, top management teams, and boards*. Oxford University Press.

Finlay, L. (2002). Negotiating the swamp: The opportunity and challenges of reflexivity in research practice. *Qualitative Research, 2,* 209–230.

Goffman, E. (1983). The interaction order. *American Sociological Review, 48,* 1–17.

Goodstein, J., Gautam, K., & Boeker, W. (1994). The effects of board size and diversity on strategic change. *Strategic Management Journal, 15*(3), 241–250.

Goodwin, C. (1994). Professional vision. *American Anthropologist, 96*(3), 606–633.

Gover, L., Halinski, M., & Duxbury, L. (2016). Is it just me? Exploring perceptions of organizational culture change. *British Journal of Management, 27,* 567–582.

Gylfe, P., Franck, H., Lebaron, C., & Mantere, S. (2016). Video methods in strategy research: Focusing on embodied cognition. *Strategic Management Journal, 37,* 133–148.

Hambrick, D. C. (2007). Upper echelons theory: An update. *Academy of Management Review, 32*(2), 334–343.

Hambrick, D. C., Humphrey, S. E., & Gupta, A. (2015). Structural interdependence within top management teams: A key moderator of upper echelons predictions. *Strategic Management Journal, 36*(3), 449–461.

Hambrick, D. C., & Mason, P. A. (1984). Upper Echelons: The organizations as a reflection of its top management. *Academy of Management Review, 9*(2), 193–206.

Headland, T., Pike, K., & Harris, M. (1990). *Emics and etics: The insider/outsider debate*. Sage.

Heath, C., & Hindmarsh, J. (2002). Qualitative research in action. In T. May (Ed.), *Qualitative research in practice* (pp. 99–121). Sage.

Hill, C. W., & Snell, S. A. (1988). External control, corporate strategy, and firm performance in research-intensive industries. *Strategic Management Journal, 9*(6), 577–590.

Iedema, R., Merrick, E. T., Rajbhandari, D., Gardo, A., Stirling, A., & Herkes, R. (2009). Viewing the taken-for-granted from under a different aspect: A video-based method in pursuit of patient safety. *International Journal of Multiple Research Approaches, 3*(3), 290–301.

Jarrett, M., & Liu, F. (2018). "Zooming with": A participatory approach to video ethnography in organizational studies. *Organizational Research Methods, 21,* 366–385.

Jarzabkowski, P., Burke, G., & Spee, P. (2015). Constructing spaces for strategic work: A multimodal perspective. *British Journal of Management, 26,* 26–47.

Kisfalvi, V., & Pitcher, P. (2003). Doing what feels right: The influence of CEO character and emotions on top management team dynamics. *Journal of Management Inquiry, 12*(1), 42–66.

Kisfalvi, V., Sergi, V., & Langley, A. (2016). Managing and mobilizing micro-dynamics to achieve behavioral integration in top management teams. *Long Range Planning, 49*(4), 427–446.

Knight, D., Pearce, C. L., Smith, K. G., Olian, J. D., Sims, H. P., Smith, K. A., et al. (1999). Top management team diversity, group process, and strategic consensus. *Strategic Management Journal, 20*(5), 445–465.

Knoblauch, H., & Schnettler, B. (2012). Videography: Analysing video data as a 'focused' ethnographic and hermeneutical exercise. *Qualitative Research, 12*(3), 334–356.

Lahlou, S. (2011). How can we capture the subject's perspective? An evidence-based approach for the social scientist. *Social Science Information, 50*(4), 607–655.

LeBaron, C., Jarzabkowski, P., Pratt, M. G., & Fetzer, G. (2018). An introduction to video methods in organizational research. *Organizational Research Methods, 21,* 239–260.

Leonard-Barton, D. (1990). A dual methodology for case studies: Synergistic use of a longitudinal single site with replicated multiple sites. *Organization Science, 1*(3), 248–266.

Liu, D., Fisher, G., & Chen, G. (2018). CEO attributes and firm performance: A sequential mediation process model. *Academy of Management Annals, 12*(2), 789–816.

Liu, F., & Maitlis, S. (2014). Emotional dynamics and strategizing processes: A study of strategic conversations in top team meetings. *Journal of Management Studies, 51,* 202–234.

Maitlis, S., & Lawrence, T. B. (2003). Orchestral manoeuvres in the dark: Understanding failure in organizational strategizing. *Journal of Management Studies, 40*(1), 109–139.

Markee, N. (2013). Emic and etic in qualitative research. In *The encyclopedia of applied linguistics* (pp. 1–4). Blackwell.

Morris, M. W., Leung, K., Ames, D., & Lickel, B. (1999). Views from inside and outside: Integrating emic and etic insights about culture and justice judgment. *Academy of Management Review, 24*(4), 781–796.

Paterson, M., & Glass, M. R. (2015). The world through Glass: Developing novel methods with wearable computing for urban videographic research. *Journal of Geography in Higher Education, 39*(2), 275–287.

Paterson, M., & Glass, M. R. (2020). Seeing, feeling, and showing 'bodies-in-place': Exploring reflexivity and the multisensory body through videography. *Social and Cultural Geography, 21*(1), 1–24.

Pike, K. (1967). Language in relation to a unified theory of the structure of human behavior. In *Language in relation to a unified theory of the structure of human behavior* (Vol. 24). De Gruyter, Inc.

Pink, S., Sumartojo, S., Lupton, D., & Heyes LaBond, C. (2017). Empathetic technologies: Digital materiality and video ethnography. *Visual Studies, 32*(4), 371–381.

Pitcher, P., & Smith, A. D. (2001). Top management team heterogeneity: Personality, power, and proxies. *Organization Science, 12*(1), 1–18.

Poyner, R. (2008). *Video ethnography.* https://www.iconeye.com/opinion/icon-of-the-month/item/3455-video-ethnography.

Rouleau, L., de Rond, M., & Musca, G. (2014). From the ethnographic turn to new forms of organizational ethnography. *Journal of Organizational Ethnography, 3*(1), 2–9.

Smets, M., Burke, G., Jarzabkowski, P., & Spee, P. (2011). Charting new territory for organizational ethnography: Insights from a team-based video ethnography. *Journal of Organizational Ethnography, 3*(1), 10–26.

Smets, M., Jarzabkowski, P., Burke, G. T., & Spee, P. (2015). Reinsurance trading in Lloyds of London: Balancing conflicting yet complementary logics in practice. *Academy of Management Journal, 58*(3), 932–970.

Smith, J. (1994). Towards reflexive practice: Engaging participants as co-researchers or co-analysts in psychological inquiry. *Journal of Community and Applied Social Psychology, 4,* 253–260.

Streeck, J., Goodwin, C., & LeBaron, C. (2011). *Embodied interaction: Language and body in the material world.* Cambridge University Press.

Vaara, E., Kleymann, B., & Seristö, H. (2004). Strategies as discursive constructions: The case of airline alliances. *Journal of Management Studies, 41*(1), 1–35.

Van Maanen, J. (2011). Ethnography as work: Some rules of engagement. *Journal of Management Studies, 48*(1), 218–234.

Vardaman, J., Amis, J., Gondo, M. (2010). Real-time cases. In A. J. Mills, G. Durepos, & E. Wiebe (Eds.), *Encyclopedia of case study research* (pp. 784–786). Sage.

Walsh, J. P., Tushman, M. L., Kimberly, J. R., Starbuck, B., & Ashford, S. (2007). On the relationship between research and practice: Debate and reflections. *Journal of Management Inquiry, 16,* 128–154.

Wiersema, M. F., & Bantel, K. A. (1992). Top management team demography and corporate strategic change. *Academy of Management Journal, 35*(1), 91–121.

CHAPTER 9

Complementing Video-Ethnography: The Uses and Potential of Mundane Data Collected on Social Media

Viviane Sergi and Claudine Bonneau

Abstract In this chapter, we argue that paying attention to the mundane aspects of work enriches our understanding of individuals' lived experience in organizations. While capturing these mundane aspects can be carried through video-ethnography, we propose that mundane data found on social media might also lead to such investigation. Using examples from our previous work, we explore how mundane data found on social media can reveal dimensions of work practices. We then show that it can offer a valuable contribution to video-ethnographic methods.

Keywords Mundane data · Social media · Workplace practices · Senses · Affect

V. Sergi (✉) · C. Bonneau
ESG UQAM, Montréal, QC, Canada
e-mail: sergi.viviane@uqam.ca

C. Bonneau
e-mail: bonneau.claudine@uqam.ca

S. Grosjean and F. Matte (eds.), *Organizational Video-Ethnography Revisited*, https://doi.org/10.1007/978-3-030-65551-8_9

9.1 Introduction

In this chapter, we suggest that data collected on mainstream social media, such as Twitter and Instagram, can offer valuable complements to video-ethnography. While in the recent years, virtual and digital ethnography practices have been more widely discussed (e.g., Hine 2015; Abidin and De Seta 2020), just like visual methodologies in general (e.g., Pink 2012), we contend that the potential of social media to deepen these methods still remain to be addressed in greater detail. In our chapter, we discuss how posts voluntarily generated by users on social media constitute what can be labeled "mundane data." Mundane data refers to the data generated in the flow of the everyday activities. This kind of data abound on social media, where expressive activities generate short snippets of digital data that are deeply anchored in the daily experience of users. Pervasiveness of mainstream social media in all spheres of daily activities, including work, means they are "increasingly implicated in all kinds of workplace phenomena that are within the areas of interest of organizational scholars" (Leonardi and Vaast 2017: 151) and that they are a site where the mundane experience of work can be explored.

Our chapter develops two main arguments. Directly influenced by the practice perspective (especially as defined by Nicolini 2013; also Gherardi 2017) and by workplace studies (Schmidt 2016; Star and Strauss 1999) we first argue that what belongs to "mundane life" is especially relevant and well-suited to gain an understanding into dimensions of work that tend to be less visible, such as affective, sensory and experiential dimensions of work practices. Echoing Shortt's study on liminal spaces at work (2015), we think that paying attention to the mundane aspects of work enriches our understanding of the lived experience of individuals in organizations. Hence, we should not be fooled by the mundane character of the ordinary experience at work—made of emotions, gestures, material challenges, claims for recognition, self-expression, reflections, and in situ bricolage, among others. If this mundane experience may constitute a large part of what is happening at work and in organization, on a daily basis, we stress that it is also the exact site where practices are born, developed and refined or modified. Indeed, definitions of practice offered by Reckwitz (2002), Schatzki (2001) or Nicolini (2013), widely mobilized in organization studies, all in one way or another stress that practice is made of knowledge, relationships, materiality, temporal concerns, embodied experience and power.

However, this position poses its own challenge: that of capturing these mundane aspects. If such an inquiry can be carried through video-ethnography, we propose that mundane data found on social media might also lead to such an investigation. This second argument echoes Pink et al.'s (2017) call for studies into mundane data related to other social practices that are reconfigured by digitalization. Our previous work (Sergi and Bonneau 2016; Bonneau and Sergi 2018; Bonneau et al., n.d.) has led us to recognize that the kind of visual and textual material shared on Twitter and Instagram (or other social media platforms) offers entry points to investigate dimensions that all refer to what practices are. After explaining how mundane data found on social media can reveal these dimensions, we show that it can offer a valuable contribution to video-ethnographic methods in three ways. Firstly, it can feed in situ video-ethnographic data collection, by providing complimentary data on dimensions that are already explored through a video-ethnographic approach. Secondly, it can prolong connection with fieldwork, even expanding the site of the video-ethnographic inquiry by offering access to distributed phenomena. Indeed, social media can act as a "digital third place" or "post-event spaces" (Abidin and De Seta 2020) functioning in parallel or extending the workspace. As we illustrate in the coming pages, social media offer researchers the possibility to stay in touch with what might be happening in different work sites and with individuals, when they are not present in the field or even after fieldwork has been completed. Hence, we suggest that while previously one had to "be there" and spend time in one organization to develop a sense of its mundane fabric, nowadays, given the penetration of social media in daily practices of an important number of individuals, these spaces represent a rich site to explore this subjective and experiential side of organizations. Finally, it allows researchers to access and document important dimensions of work practices, including aesthetic, affective and embodied facets of work and other experiences, that would be difficult to capture through video-ethnography.

9.2 Mainstream Social Media as Windows into the Mundane Aspects of Work and Life

A growing number of organizations use "enterprise social media" (ESM) platforms such as Yammer and Workplace by Facebook to foster knowledge sharing and informal communication between their employees

(Oostervink et al. 2016). These organizations provide guidance to their members on how to use these platforms in their work. In addition to these mandatory (or prescribed) uses, employees who come to work with their personal mobile phones can use them to access mainstream social media platforms (e.g., Facebook, Twitter, Instagram, Snapchat and TikTok), even if access is restricted on computers provided by their employers. They can turn to this parallel channel to voluntarily share aspects of their daily work, in ways that differ than what is formally expected from them on corporate platforms. Workers performing more conventional work (e.g., farmers or bakers) might also use them even if they do not make use of digital tools to conduct their work. Furthermore, the pervasiveness of social media is directly linked with the current omnipresence of mobile phones, which usually come with cameras. As digital photography has become ubiquitous, any aspect of contemporary life, including work, can become visual content.

In this context, considering social media means studying both the textual and visual material that is shared on these platforms. Our previous work has allowed us to explore that people use mainstream social media to share not only material (thoughts, impressions, experiences, moods, etc.) linked to their personal life, but also related to their working life (Sergi and Bonneau 2016; Bonneau and Sergi 2018; Bonneau et al., n.d.), a practice that we have named working out loud (WOL). While our initial impulse for conducting this research was to explore how workers use social media in the course of their work, we did not start our investigation with an idea about what, exactly, people may be sharing on social media like Twitter and Instagram. Over time, as we collected and analyzed data, we discovered that workers share a variety of apparently banal details about their own experience of work (which includes the embodied and temporal aspects of the work, and elements relating to the atmosphere in which they work). For instance, we found posts in which a person is sharing her reflections on an aspect of her work while showing her work environment. Another presents his work-in-progress or shares his emotional state following an event at work. In most of the data collected, we noticed that people were fundamentally referring to their ordinary experience at work and sharing banal observations or reflections, hence our labeling of this data as mundane. As Hand underlines, the number of mundane images that can be found on social media "might be cited as evidence of the increasing documentation of everyday life as a generalized condition" (2012: 14). In our view, this general observation points to the untapped potential of social media to explore the mundane aspects of work and life in organization. However, our point is not so much about the occurrence of these elements, but about their newfound visibility via social media—and, more significantly here, about their possible richness as source of data about the experience of work, work settings and work practices that can complement approaches based on video-ethnography.

What belongs to the mundane tends to be de-valorized, and hence neglected by researchers (e.g., Brekhus 2000; Woolgar and Neyland 2014; Ybema et al. 2009), because of this "ordinary" character. However, studying the mundane elements of life has a long tradition in social sciences, especially in sociology and in anthropology. Especially in relation to work, the mundane has been at the heart of some research traditions, such as ethnomethodology (Garfinkel 1967) and workplace studies (Heath et al. 2000). Interestingly, we can note that most of these studies have relied on the ethnographic tradition to pursue their inquiry, which may or may not have to do initially with mundane aspects; but given the kind of data collected, these studies have been able to capture ordinary facets of human activity. For example, sociologists of work associated with workplace studies have used ethnographic approaches to study invisible work (e.g., Star and Strauss 1999), especially inquiring into workers' practices that are "utterly dull and uninteresting" (Schmidt 2016)—in other words, mundane. This pioneering work—which often mobilized actual conversations between workers and photos of workplaces—has put forward a fully situated understanding of work, shedding light on the daily interactions and the sophisticated intertwinement between people and tools that are part of the ordinary accomplishment of work. In doing so, these studies have shown that far from being uninteresting, the mundane, the informal and the less visible are in fact a rich gateway to document the practices of work in various settings. For their part, researchers working at the intersection of workplace studies and computer-supported cooperative work (CSCW) have also relied on detailed ethnographic studies of work collectives to uncover "articulation work"—the "supra" type of work that needs to be performed in order to support and accomplish the "orderliness" of work (Strauss 1985; Schmidt and Bannon 1992; Schmidt 2011)—and to understand its imbrication with material artifacts. While studies of professional work have long put emphasis on judgmental and interpretive work, Suchman and her colleagues have uncovered the mundane practice aspects of articulation work and showed how technology contributes to this process (Suchman et al. 1999; Suchman 2000).

Studying and understanding work today, even in its ordinary experience, require in most circumstances to take into consideration its intertwinement with technology. As Orlikowski and Scott (2016) underline, "all work is today being reconfigured in relation to digital technologies, and so it is important for us to draw attention to and craft accounts of the critical issues that this raises" (p. 89). Indeed, in a context where these tools are becoming more and more present in workplaces, ethnographic practice has been reinvented to enter new fields of inquiry, such as social media (Hine 2015). Ethnographic researchers and methods need to be mobile and flexible to adapt to the evolution of the work environment. Combining physical and digital ethnography can be a fruitful way to account for the contemporary forms of "multi-modal working practices" (Hine 2017) involving people who constantly switch between offline and online work and communication, such as distributed teams and digital nomads. However, a majority of social media studies in relation to work focus more on the technological side of this phenomenon, and less on what is produced with and via the imbrication of these tools in daily enactment of work. In a context where the boundaries between work and non-work are blurring, we consider that it is important to explore what might appear as belonging more to the informal side of organizational life, especially since this mundane aspect has found new ways of expressing itself. This is where that video-ethnography reveals all of its potential—but also, as we will discuss, mundane data shared on social media.

By definition, social media are tied to the mundane and daily life, as they are meant to share these very experiences. In this sense, they can be seen as the par excellence site to access what is ordinary, what seems inconsequential and banal, details of work and organizational life. We argue that there are strong parallels between what is experienced at an individual level on a mundane basis, and what characterized social media. Indeed, both are tied around the notion of ephemerality. On the one side, mundane experience refers to what happens as action is unfolding, may be diffuse and difficult to put in words and may be related to sensorial perception or personal experience. On the other side, social media are fully embedded in daily life, may use words, but more and more rely on visual, even video content and offer the possibility to evoke many elements pertaining to what is lived in a single post. These parallels justify our proposal that social media represent relevant and rich site to access and capture these ephemeral facets that make up the experience of life and work.

Also, temporally speaking, what happens on social media is firmly located in the present moment, making it at least partially revelatory of what is being experienced by users who are sharing material. Our studies of WOL have already shown that by turning to public social media that are not controlled by their employers, workers in a variety of settings make their work more visible (Sergi and Bonneau 2016), and that this visibilization is both a material and a discursive process. This inquiry allowed us to show that social media are being used by workers to shed light on what is taking place in the backstage of work, elements that are usually left in the shadows of formal discussions of work. Furthermore, if ethnographic approaches in general grant researchers with access, at least partially, to this backstage of work, it does not guarantee access to all facets of the experience of work, nor to access at the right moment to catch ephemeral and fugitive elements than nonetheless may be highly relevant to understand work. This might especially be the case for elements that relate to affective, aesthetic or sensorial dimensions of work which are by definition complex, embodied and may be difficult to put in words. This is where elements pertaining to work shared on social media, albeit materializing through very short text, accompanied or not by visual content, might offer insights for video-ethnographers. Let us now explore in greater detail the ways in which these mundane data on social media can offer valuable material for video-ethnographers.

9.3 The Contribution of Mundane Data to Video-Ethnography

As its name implies and its simplest definition, video-ethnography combines ethnography with video capture. Recorded data can adopt a wide range of form, documenting a multitude of phenomena and especially dimensions of work, and it would be impossible to be exhaustive in this chapter. While the possibilities of video-ethnography, especially to access and observe affective, sensorial and embodied aspects of the experience of being at work, are vast, this approach still rest on the notion of presence. This raises the question of not only being there, but being there at the right time. This is where mundane data collected on social media, and especially data pertaining to work experience, can be generative for video-ethnographers. In the next sections, we highlight three of these potential contributions of social media data. The two first contributions are of empirical and methodological nature and can therefore be applied to any video-ethnographic approach. First, social media can feed the in situ data collection process by providing more data about dimensions already investigated by video-ethnography. Second, social media can broaden the research site by allowing the video-ethnographer to extend his presence and pursue his work through different channels, temporalities and places. The third contribution is rather of theoretical-empirical, since it is more concerned with researchers whose studies are rooted in the practice perspective, highlighting that mundane data collected on social media can allow them to access and document different dimensions related to the multidimensional concept of practice.

9.3.1 Feeding in Situ Video-Ethnographic Data Collection

This is the most obvious contribution of mundane data collected on social media. Given that people who are part of a work setting where a video-ethnography is being conducted, considering what their organization shares on social media might already be included in the inquiry process. Although these data can be quite useful, depending on the focal point of the video-ethnography, this is not primarily what we refer to when we talk of mundane data. Rather, what we designate by "mundane data" are the posts on mainstream social media, as produced by workers in a personal fashion. Our previous work on working out loud allowed us to discover that people in a wide array of occupations will turn to social media to share a moment of their daily life, in a manner that does not appear as required by their work. For example, in the Instagram post shown in Fig. 9.1, the second author of this chapter shares a snippet of her reflection on an ongoing research project, while making it obvious that she was working while being on vacations.[1] The

[1] For copyright reasons, we were not able to include any of the posts that we have collected in the course of our research on working out loud. We hence offer this example produced by one of us, as we also, from time to time, engage in working out loud on social media. It should be noted that this post was not included in our data collection, but was chosen to provide an illustration for this chapter.

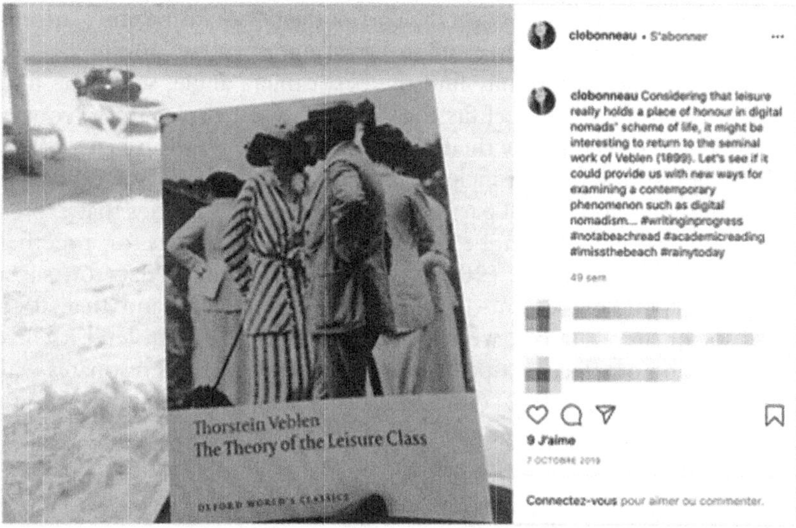

Fig. 9.1 Social media can offer glimpses in how people view their own experience

whole post, combining photo and textual elements (including the hashtags, like #writinginprogress) illustrate how such posts offer to workers and to researchers alike glimpses in how people view their own experience of work. As such, social media platforms function like instruments that make visible: as Le Breton (2006) reminds us, in many instances it is instruments that make visible aspects that would otherwise be almost impossible to see, such as galaxies far away or microscopic cells.

Considering these mundane data can feed video-ethnography by helping the video-ethnographer notice aspects that may be relevant to the experience of work, hence sharpening his eye and eliciting questions worth asking to workers. Asking workers about what may have motivated them to share something related to their work experience may help researchers to gain understanding both of the specific work setting in which they are located, but also of the person's relation to his work. Furthermore, posting on social media, especially on Instagram, should not be taken for granted, as each post can be highly customized by the user and his or her personal use of each platform. While not necessarily requiring significant effort, the visual narration of work activities on social media implies a form of work on the part of the person using the platform, and a series of choices. For example, creating a post on Instagram may lead users to have to carefully find the best camera angle, select the filter for their photo that they feel fits the best with what they want to convey, to craft a text to accompany their photo (although a post can be wordless) and to choose hashtags to include. Text caption, emoji, choice of filter, comments, and more are all part of a post, and are specificities that express something and hence can be analyzed, either separately or together. Following Gherardi et al. (2019), given that mundane data on social media are about expression—and even self-expression—and that affect leaves sociomaterial traces, we consider that these data can lend itself to an exploration of affective aspects of work experience. This resonates with how Postill and Pink (2012) describe "social media ethnography" as a way to zoom into the affective intensities of interactions online and offline.

9.3.2 Expanding the Site of Video-Ethnography

Not only can mundane data offer complementary data in itself to researchers, but this material can serve as way to deepen the video-ethnography by providing cues that can orient the video-ethnographer's eye, extending it beyond what might have initially been the scope of the researcher by making visible otherwise unidentifiable issues. But the potential for extension is not limited to dimensions or aspects to be included in the study, but is also very much spatial. Social media offer the possibility of following action where is it going and going on, making it easier to travel with participants to the sites where phenomena are happening. In the context of the growing digitalization of work and life, the notion of site as a single place may be questioned, pursuing the questioning opened in the 90s in light of the intensification of globalization of a variety of issues. This had led Marcus (1995) to coin the term "multi-sited ethnography," a term that has since been at the fore of debates (Falzon 2016). But beyond these debates, mobility on the part of the ethnographer seems to be more and more needed. At the same time, such mobility may be difficult to perform, as these other relevant sites for a given study may be difficult for researchers to access, in terms of distance, resources or effort required to do so. If interviews can allow researchers to learn about what might be happening elsewhere, mundane data found on social media may facilitate the work of following what is happening, hence extending the video-ethnography data collection. The snippet-size of mundane data found on social media cannot of course replace ethnographic involvement, be it on the move or not, but it might still offer the possibility of looking into what might be taking place in a physical location different from where the researcher is located.

Also, given the prevalence of visual content and material shared on these sites, social media lend themselves especially well to methodologies in which participants are actively involved. As Wilhoit (2017) reminds us about photo and video methods in general:

> [these methods] allow researchers to communicate with participants in different ways, providing prompts for discussion, adding a temporal dimension to interviewing, allowing participants to create meaning through different modalities, and incorporating more senses and ways of knowing into the interview setting. (2017: 459)

However, whereas other methodologies will involve participants from the start in a research project, by equipping them with cameras for example (Wilhoit developed such an approach, that they call participant viewpoint ethnography; see also Wilhoit and Kisselburg 2016), visual studies of social media can also be conducted by the researcher, in connection with the person using social media to share material regarding his or her work.

9.3.3 Documenting Dimensions of Practice

Our previous work on social media reveals that when workers engage in working out loud on social media, they are talking, in visual terms, about what they are encountering while at work, evoking elements linked to the daily accomplishment of work. These elements may be linked to the mundane side of organizational life, conceptually, they represent "entry points" into the practices and the accomplishment of work. Table 9.1 presents the experiential dimensions exposed by individuals on Twitter and Instagram that we have up to now documented in our ongoing study of people working out loud on social media.

For each category identified, we propose connections with a larger conceptual dimension. Hence, each of these categories can be seen as a "springboard" toward documenting different conceptual dimensions of work. This echoes Pink et al. (2017) who, in line with other researchers, consider "the mundane as the landing site where phenomena such as technology and power can be studied" (p. 3). Given the list of elements

Table 9.1 Emerging repertoire of categories of posts related to the experience of work

Category	*Sub-categories*	*Work dimension that could be studied with this category*
1. Embodied experience	1.1 Sensorial 1.2 Physical	Knowledge
2. Intensity of work	2.1 Difficulties and challenges 2.2 Emotions and feelings	Emotions
3. Materiality	3.1 Setup and environment 3.2 Tools	Sociomateriality
4. Backstage	4.1 Context that is rarely seen 4.2 Mundane aspects of work	Invisible dimensions of work
5. Temporality	5.1 Working at unexpected time 5.2 Temporal ordering	Time
6. Presence	6.1 Work-life boundaries 6.2 Giving presence to women 6.3 Unexpected presence	Professional identity and power issues
7. Atmosphere	7.1 Life at work 7.2 Fun and informal	Ambiance and aesthetics

identified as sub-categories, this table can also support data collection, helping in the selection of posts through the identification of dimensions they render visible.

This mundane and visual material might lead us to deepen the relationships between practice and affect, given their theoretical proximity. As Gherardi suggests, "[t]hrough the theoretical framework of practice, we can analyse the 'doing-in-situation,' and the theoretical framework of affect directs attention to the collective circulation of feeling and of an atmosphere that adds to practices the dimension of intensity that emanates from but exceeds the assembling of bodies, activities and materialities" (2017: 351).

9.4 Ethical Considerations

It should however be noted that including the content voluntarily produced on social media by workers comes with a number of methodological and ethical questions. First, these platforms continuously develop and change over time, which makes it difficult to stay aware of their specificities. Therefore, researchers who engage with them will be "best situated to understand its developing affordances and norms" (Laestadius 2017: 589), and should keep up with their development. Second, the analysis of user-generated content on social media poses specific challenges, given their multiple interpretive possibilities. This is where the imbrication with video-ethnography can prove highly relevant, as the presence over time in a context allows relationships to be built, facilitating conversations with the people regarding the content related to work that they have shared on social media. Indeed, in addition to "traditional" form of interviews, there are methods that allow for the co-analysis of data between researchers and participants. "Trace interviews" (Dubois and Ford 2015) involve the joint exploration and discussion of social media posts with the participants who published them. This process has also an ethical benefit, since participants become fully aware of what researchers collected, "therefore increasing trust and making the notion of 'informed consent' more meaningful" (Latzko-Toth et al. 2017: 210). Although the kind of posts we have discussed here are made available publicly, participants should be duly and well informed that what they post may be considered in the research.

As noted by Abidin and De Seta (2020: 10) regarding the challenges faced by digital ethnographers, "the most widely recommended remedy to assuage epistemological anxieties, participatory doubts and ethical dilemmas is self-reflexivity." Interestingly, another potential we see with the use of social media mundane data relates to the researcher's reflexivity. Indeed, if the researcher takes time to pay attention to her own affective reactions to the material shared on social media, it can become a way to interrogate her assumptions as a researcher and possibly implicit framings about work and/or the context where the study is taking place. When considering a post on an ordinary aspect of work, how do we react? What initially captures our attention? What do we find less interesting, in a post? How do we perceive what is presented, what does this content elicit in us, in terms of affective and sensorial reaction? Do we experience surprise or shock, even on a banal scale—or not? These reactions can hence become cues or objects to reflect on, saying something about us as researchers, about our choices in the design and practice of research and potentially contributing in enriching our understanding of phenomena (Devereux 1967; Kisfalvi 2006; Sergi and Hallin 2011).

9.5 Concluding Remarks

We believe that researchers opting for video-ethnography can gain a lot by including social media as a site of investigation, as it can inform significant research on a broad range of topics related to their interests. As Table 9.1 illustrated, while the kind of mundane data we have discussed here may be quite “small” in size and fragmentary, they can display a wide variety of elements related to the experience of work. Connected with other data collection approaches, including video-ethnography, such posts can become generative for researchers already paying attention to the minutiae of daily life and practices. Furthermore, as we have briefly explored in this chapter, we consider that mundane data may be the “second-best” approach, after all forms of continuous presence in the field belonging to video-ethnography, to visually capture what is happening in daily life at work and in organizational settings. The mundane nature of this data attests of its proximity to what is experienced, while the fact that they are voluntarily produced by individuals confers them a form of validity.

Already in 2001, Green was shedding light on the mundane production of virtual reality, showing that everyday labor and laborers where key in articulating of technology and culture associated to the experience of virtual reality. “As such, they [the workers making virtual reality happen for participants] crucially embody the junctures of techno-cultural production and consumption by bringing together bodies and technologies, and reciprocally transforming technology into culture, and culture into technology” (2001: 89). She underlined that considering “relatively unremarkable activities” could open the door to an investigation of social mechanisms, especially those at play at the interface of culture and technology. A similar argument has been made by Gregg, who for her part stressed how political discourses and forces ultimately shape the mundane: “[s]ituating the mundane as the site for analysis forces us to grapple with the concrete ways political discourses shape experience” (2004: 379). More recently, Wolf (2016) discussed how individuals watching DIY videos on YouTube were, in doing so, evaluating their own capacities and were engaging in identity work—albeit in a minute form—an idea that we also proposed based on our study of working out loud on Twitter (Sergi and Bonneau 2016). These studies show that activities and practices that appear very banal can offer a relevant starting point to study the complex imbrication and articulation of the social and the material, a starting point from which it is possible to "scale up" or "zoom out," toward a reflection on broader phenomena. Video-ethnography do allow to document in a detailed way what is happening at work and while people are going about their ordinary activities, and in this chapter, our main argument has been about the complementary nature of mundane data found on social media. Material found on social media like Instagram and Twitter may seem banal, but we believe that it can allow researchers to, at the same time, delve into the intricacies of experimenting work and reflect on how social media may contribute in reconfiguring some facets of work practices.

References

Abidin, C., & De Seta, G. (2020). Private messages from the field. *Journal of Digital Social Research, 2*(1), 1–19.

Bonneau, C., Endrissat, N., & Sergi, V. (n.d.). Social media as a new workspace: How working out loud (re)materializes work. In *Artefacts, materiality and practices*. Palgrave.

Bonneau, C., & Sergi, V. (2018). *Sharing and accessing the mundane dimensions of work on social media: The role of mediated visibility for workers and researchers*. Presented at the panel "More than meets the eyes: the lens of visibility in Internet research". Conference of the Association of Internet Researchers (AoIR2018), Montréal (Canada).

Brekhus, W. (2000). A mundane manifesto. *Journal of Mundane Behavior, 1*(1), 89–105.

Devreux, G. (1967). *From anxiety to method in the behavioural sciences*. Mouton & Co.

Dubois, E., & Ford, H. (2015). Qualitative political communication| trace interviews: An actor-centered approach. *International Journal of Communication, 9*(25).

Falzon, M. A. (2016). Introduction: Multi-sited ethnography: Theory, praxis and locality in contemporary research. In M.-A. Falzon (Ed.), *Multi-sited ethnography: Theory, praxis and locality in contemporary research* (pp. 1–23). Routledge.

Garfinkel, H. (1967). *Studies in ethnomethodology*. Prentice-Hall.

Gherardi, S. (2017). One turn… and now another one: Do the turn to practice and the turn to affect have something in common? *Management Learning, 48*(3), 345–358.

Gherardi, S., Murgia, A., Bellè, E., Miele, F., & Carreri, A. (2019). Tracking the sociomaterial traces of affect at the crossroads of affect and practice theories. *Qualitative Research in Organizations and Management, 14*(3), 295–316.

Green, N. (2001). How everyday life became virtual: Mundane work at the juncture of production and consumption. *Journal of Consumer Culture, 1*(1), 73–92.

Gregg, M. (2004). A mundane voice. *Cultural Studies, 18*(2–3), 363–383.

Hand, M. (2012). *Ubiquitous photography*. Polity.

Heath, C., Knoblauch, H., & Luff, P. (2000). Technology and social interaction: The emergence of 'workplace studies'. *The British Journal of Sociology, 51*(2), 299–320.

Hine, C. (2015). *Ethnography for the Internet: Embedded, embodied and everyday*. Bloomsbury Publishing.

Hine, C. (2017). *Research methods for digital work: Innovative methods for studying distributed and multi-modal working practices*. Retrieved January 5, 2017, from http://www.ias.surrey.ac.uk/workshops/workpractices/cfp.php.

Kisfalvi, V. (2006). Subjectivity and emotions as sources of insight in an ethnographic case study: A tale of the field. *Management, 9*(3), 117–135.

Laestadius, L. (2017). Instagram. In A. Quan-Haase & L. Sloan (Eds.), *The SAGE handbook of social media research methods* (pp. 573–592). Sage.

Latzko-Toth, G., Bonneau, C., & Millette, M. (2017). Small data, thick data: Thickening strategies for trace-based social media research. In A. Quan-Haase & L. Sloan (Eds.), *The SAGE handbook of social media research methods* (pp. 199–214). Sage.

Le Breton, D. (2006). *La saveur du monde: une anthropologie des sens*. Éd. Métailié.

Leonardi, P. M., & Vaast, E. (2017). Social media and their affordances for organizing: A review and agenda for research. *The Academy of Management Annals, 11*(1), 150–188.

Marcus, G. E. (1995). Ethnography in/of the world system: The emergence of multi-sited ethnography. *Annual Review of Anthropology, 24,* 95–117.

Nicolini, D. (2013). *Practice theory, work, and organization: An introduction*. Oxford University Press.

Oostervink, N., Agterberg, M., & Huysman, M. (2016). Knowledge sharing on enterprise social media: Practices to cope with institutional complexity. *Journal of Computer-Mediated Communication, 21*(2), 156–176.

Orlikowski, W. J., & Scott, S. V. (2016). Digital work: A research agenda. In B. Czarniawska (Ed.), *A research agenda for management and organization studies* (pp. 88–96). Edward Elgar Publishing.

Pink, S. (2012). *Advances in visual methodology*. Sage.

Pink, S., Sumartojo, S., Lupton, D., & Heyes La Bond, C. (2017). Mundane data: The routines, contingencies and accomplishments of digital living. *Big Data & Society, 4*(1), 1–12.

Postill, J., & Pink, S. (2012). Social media ethnography: The digital researcher in a messy web. *Media International Australia, 145*, 123–134.

Reckwitz, A. (2002). Toward a theory of social practices: A development in culturalist theorizing. *European Journal of Social Theory, 5*(2), 243–263.

Schatzki, T. R. (2001). Introduction—Practice theory. In T. R. Schatzki, K. Knorr-Cetina, & E. von Savigny (Eds.), *The practice turn in contemporary theory* (pp. 1–14). London: Routledge.

Schmidt, K. (2011). *Cooperative work and coordinative practices*. Springer.

Schmidt, K. (2016). Reflections on the visibility and invisibility of work. In *Boundary objects and beyond: Working with Leigh Star* (pp. 345–349). MIT Press.

Schmidt, K., & Bannon, L. (1992). Taking CSCW seriously: Supporting articulation work. *Computer Supported Cooperative Work, 1*(1), 7–40.

Sergi, V., & Bonneau, C. (2016). Making mundane work visible on social media: A CCO investigation of working out loud on Twitter. *Communication Research and Practice, 2*(3), 378–406.

Sergi, V., & Hallin, A. (2011). Thick performances, not just thick descriptions: The processual nature of qualitative research. *Qualitative Research in Organization and Management, 6*(2), 191–208.

Shortt, H. (2015). Liminality, space and the importance of 'transitory dwelling places' at work. *Human Relations, 68*(4), 633–658.

Star, S. L., & Strauss, A. (1999). Layers of silence, arenas of voice: The ecology of visible and invisible work. *Computer Supported Cooperative Work, 8*(1–2), 9–30.

Strauss, A. (1985). Work and the division of labour. *Sociological Quarterly, 26*(1), 1–19.

Suchman, L. (2000). Making a case: Knowledge and routine work in document production. In P. Luff, J. Hindmarsh, & C. Heath (Eds.), *Workplace studies: Recovering work practice and informing system design* (pp. 29–45). Cambridge University Press.

Suchman, L., Blomberg, J., Orr, J., & Trigg, R. (1999). Reconstructing technologies as social practice. *American Behavioral Scientist Behavioral Scientist, 34*(3), 392–408.

Wilhoit, E. D. (2017). Photo and video methods in organizational and managerial communication research. *Management Communication Quarterly, 31*(3), 447–466.

Wilhoit, E. D., & Kisselburgh, L. G. (2016). Through the eyes of the participant: Making connections between researcher and subject with participant viewpoint ethnography. *Field Methods, 28*(2), 208–226.
Wolf, C. T. (2016). DIY videos on YouTube: Identity and possibility in the age of algorithms. *First Monday, 21*(6). https://doi.org/10.5210/fm.v21i6.6787.
Woolgar, S., & Neyland, D. (2014). *Mundane governance: Ontology and accountability*. Oxford University Press.
Ybema, S., Yanow, D., Welsh, H., & Kamsteeg, F. (2009). *Organizational ethnography: Studying the complexities of everyday life*. Sage.

Index

S. Grosjean and F. Matte (eds.), *Organizational Video-Ethnography Revisited*, https://doi.org/10.1007/978-3-030-65551-8

The manufacturer's authorised representative in the EU is Springer Nature Customer Service Centre GmbH, Europaplatz 3, 69115 Heidelberg, Germany. If you have any concerns regarding our products, please contact ProductSafety@springernature.com

Printed and bound by CPI Group (UK) Ltd, Croydon, CR0 4YY
30/09/2026
02225457-0001